ARTHUR J. TOWNLEY | JUNE H. SCHMIEDER-RAMIREZ

11
ELEVENTH EDITION

School
FINANCE

— A CALIFORNIA PERSPECTIVE —

Kendall Hunt
publishing company

Pictured on cover: John Swett (1830-1913). Photo deemed public domain.

Kendall Hunt
publishing company

www.kendallhunt.com
Send all inquiries to:
4050 Westmark Drive
Dubuque, IA 52004-1840

Contents

CHAPTER 1
Financing Education in an Atmosphere of Change   1

CHAPTER 2
History of California School Finance   15

CHAPTER 3

California Education: Challenges and Opportunities   31

CHAPTER 4

Role of the Chief Business Officer   47

CHAPTER 5

Managing the Budget   59

CHAPTER 6

School District Revenue   71

CHAPTER 7

Program Budgeting and Expenditures Accounting   83

CHAPTER 8

School District Funds   95

CHAPTER 9

School Site Budgeting   103

CHAPTER 10
The Annual Audit   111

CHAPTER 11
Student Body Organizations   121

CHAPTER 12
Transportation   131

CHAPTER 13

Maintenance and Operations   141

CHAPTER 14

School Food Service Program   149

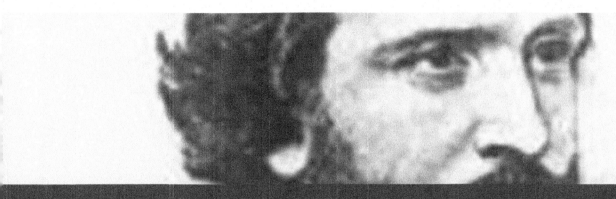

List of Figures

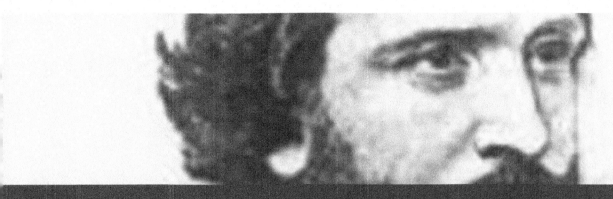

List of Tables

Introduction

John Swett was the fourth California Superintendent of Public Instruction and served from 1863 to 1867. His achievements include creating a State Board of Education and the California Teachers Association. His tenure included the upgrading of teacher training and the improvement of teacher salaries. School facilities were greatly improved under his leadership.

By the close of his term, he had abolished tuition and made attendance at public schools free for at least five months each year. He is often referred to as the father of public school education in California. It is with appreciation and to honor Swett that he has been placed on the 11th edition of this book.

California school finance resembles quantum physics in that both are extremely complex. The objective of this book is to illuminate a path through the thicket of financial terms and present the subject in a straightforward way.

California school finance has endured tremendous upheaval in the last three decades. Meeting the educational needs of an increasing and diverse student population remains a major challenge for the citizens of this state. Many school districts in California, particularly those in urban settings and those declining in enrollment, must constantly reduce some programs to meet increasing demands in others. Districts continually seek expanded resources to balance the budget and maintain a viable educational program. Among the causes of this never-ending quest are collective bargaining settlements, need for new facilities, and deteriorating assets.

For many years, California depended upon the property tax to finance schools. Districts in neighboring communities had been spending unequal amounts per student to accomplish similar educational goals. However, in a landmark case that reversed this traditional means of state school financing, the 1971 *Serrano* decision declared the property tax unconstitutional as a means of supporting public schools (*Serrano v. Priest*, upheld 18 C.3d 728, 1976), The court ruled that neither a child's place of residence nor the wealth of a community should determine financial support for the educational program.

Beginning in 1972, several school bills were passed to implement *Serrano* and, subsequently, to recover the dollars lost in the wake of Proposition 13. In 2015-2016 the per-pupil expenditure in California ranked 29th among the states. The national average was $12,572, while California was spending $11,508. The District of Columbia had the highest per pupil expenditure at $21,299, while Utah had the least at $6,911 (NEA, 2017).

The information presented in this book is as up-to-date as possible. Nevertheless, because school finance is continually evolving, any book on this topic must inevitably contain some inaccuracies, even before it can be printed. Therefore, the reader will find it necessary to keep track of developments ranging from local bond elections to state and federal legislation and court decisions affecting local school districts.

Topics included in this text are a history of school finance in California and the evolving environment of education in the state. The roles of the Chief Business Official (CBO) and essential information regarding revenues, fund accounting, income and expenditures, projections, and audits are presented. Other chapters discuss the wide-ranging responsibilities of the CBO: transportation, maintenance and operations, food services, and facilities. School site budgeting and fiscal management of student body organizations are included. Each chapter is followed by a list of key terms and a set of questions that lead the reader to review and apply what has been learned. The text closes with a glossary of school finance terms and a list of references. Accompanying materials include a workbook, masters for overhead transparencies, and PowerPoint outlines.

Financing Education in an Atmosphere of Change

If a nation expects to be ignorant and free,
it expects what never was and never will be.

(Thomas Jefferson, letter to Colonel Charles Yancy, January 6, 1816)

Introduction

With the end of the cold war in 1989, public education replaced national defense as the number one political issue. How to fix public schools was debated at local, state, and national levels during the 1990s and early 2000s. It was a major campaign issue in the presidential contest between Bush and Gore in 2000. With the election of George W. Bush, new federal legislation, No Child Left Behind (NCLB), became the national focus for improving education.

The tragic events of September 11, 2001, again shifted the nation's attention—this time from education to the war on terrorism. Soon, the terrorism challenge was followed by the war with Afghanistan and Iraq. In addition, just before the end of the first decade of the 21st century, the nation was hit with the devastating recession in 2008. Each of these historical events required enormous resources that could have gone to improve the education of students.

Although the nation had to refocus its priorities on energy and resources for the safety of the nation, education remained a major priority for parents, local communities, and the states. The 49th Annual Phi Delta Kappa/Gallup Poll (Langer Research, 2016) confirms that public schools are a priority and have strong community support. Forty-nine percent of the survey respondents gave their local community school an A or B grade. This grade was even higher by parents who had a child in a public school, where 62% gave the schools a grade of A or B.

However, when citizens were asked to grade public schools in the nation as a whole, those giving A or B dropped to 18%. In addition, a majority of the respondents disagreed with particular provisions of NCLB. These data indicate that while there is a consensus among Americans that education is a top priority, there is considerable debate about educational issues and continuing concern about unresolved problems.

Indeed, anyone who has followed educational debates in the press, attended a school board meeting, or listened to a discussion among educators knows there is little consensus on the ends of education or how to achieve them. Compounding this issue is the realization that education is "big business," with one person in five either attending or employed by a secondary or elementary school.

The purpose of this chapter is to raise educational issues that face the nation and policies where there is agreement and disagreement. The discussion centers around the value of education for the individual and the public. The issues where we lack consensus relate to linking resources to outcomes as well as funding structures that will best deliver those resources. These provocative issues provide a backdrop for discussing the great issues in educational finance.

Debates and Dilemmas in School Finance

Despite the consensus among most Americans that education is top priority, many issues remain unresolved. For example, arguments have raged for years about patterns of school district organization. How should districts and schools be organized to promote equality of educational outcomes? Should the desires of the community take precedence over those of the district, state, or nation in governance of the local school? How do concerns for competition in the global economy or pressures for school choice impact the future of schooling? What is the proper role of the federal government in K–12 education? Two issues—No Child Left Behind, approved under the presidency of George W. Bush, and Common Core, supported by President Obama, illustrate the differences between the solutions proposed by U.S. presidents to improve education. The issues also demonstrate the conflicts faced by the public in accepting the proposed solutions.

These debates grew more intense with the election of George W. Bush in 2000 and subsequent passage of the NCLB Act. The president introduced the new program and announced that bipartisan education reform was "the cornerstone of my Administration" (USDOE, n.d.). This legislation resulted in a major shift toward federal control of public education.

The federal government's role in education became a major campaign issue in the election of 2016 between Hillary Clinton and Donald Trump. Trump was critical of much of the work of the past several presidents for expanding and funding federal education programs. He strongly advocated reducing the federal government's role in education by returning more power to the states and local communities. However, no new legislation to accomplish this objective has occurred during his first year in office.

President Trump's appointment of Betsy DeVos as Secretary of Education was narrowly approved by the Senate with a tie vote between Republican and Democratic Senators. The tie was broken by the vote of the President of the Senate, Vice President Mike Pence.

Shortly after the appointment of DeVos, the president signed an executive order directing the Secretary of Education to review the department's regulations with the intent of returning more power to the states. The results of this review were not published at the time this text went to press.

Widely Accepted Concepts

Even though competing social values cloud issues of school finance, several concepts are widely accepted. These concepts include the following:

- the private and the public good of education
- local autonomy
- fiscal federalism
- funding for special needs
- equal opportunity
- efficiency

Private and Public Good of Education

There are many reasons why education is regarded as a public good. The main argument involves the benefit to society of an educated populace. An educated citizenry is better able to cast informed votes, manage personal resources, and benefit from lifelong learning. The return to society from an educated populace was thoroughly discussed in 1776 by Adam Smith in *The Wealth of Nations* and further developed by Charles Benson in 1978.

Closely tied to the argument of the value of an educated populace are the consequences of an uneducated citizenry. The major costs of welfare are well documented. In addition, studies have compared the cost of one year in prison with the cost of one year of preschool—a shocking illustration of the price of failure to fund education, especially at the pre-kindergarten level. Of course, it must be acknowledged that numerous other factors are related to crime and unemployment, including individual characteristics, early upbringing, opportunity, and determination.

Turning to education as a private good, many studies have illustrated the benefit of education over a lifetime of earnings. Furthermore, state courts have upheld the right of each individual to an education. Although an individual acquires benefits from an education, so do the nation, state, local community, employers, and taxpayers. Consequently, a debate arises as to who should pay for this benefit. Even if it is agreed that all should share the burden of financing education, further contention centers on precisely how that burden should be distributed.

Local Autonomy

Within districts, a traditional approach to budgeting has placed salary and fringe benefit decisions at the central office, allocating a limited amount to local sites for instructional supplies and supplementary services. This approach has been prevalent because the district retains the capacity to track personnel expenditures—the highest line item in the budget.

However, decentralization of school district leadership emerged as a major thrust in the 1990s as public schools sought to respond to negative public perceptions. Urban school districts, which have languished for lack of superintendents to lead them, are adopting local autonomy as a way to increase school productivity. The concept that underlies school-based management is that decisions are typically based on better information when they are made close to the level at which they are implemented.

Even though the overall purpose of local autonomy is to delegate more power to local schools, site-based management has many variations. Districts differ widely in the degree to which decentralization and local autonomy are instituted. Most approaches to decentralization involve empowerment of groups that include parents, teachers, and—at the secondary level—students. Participative management and its variants have been the subject of multitudinous conferences throughout the state.

Fiscal Federalism

The funding relationship among local, state, and federal governments has been described as a marbled layer cake that—by some miracle—works, although in a cumbersome manner. "Fiscal federalism" is the formal term for this relationship. It involves a balancing act among the levels of government. For example, in cases of wide disparity in funding for local districts, the state can step in to compensate for regional differences in amounts allocated per pupil. Similarly, the federal government may supplement budgets for special needs such as special education and compensatory education.

During several periods in the nation's history, major concern was expressed that the balance of power between the states and national government had become unbalanced. For example, during a time of war or national emergency the federal government assumes more power to tax and conduct the war. During the 1960s, concern about ensuring equal treatment across the states led to an increased federal role in social programs, including education.

During the presidencies of Richard Nixon and Ronald Reagan, the tendency was to shift power and authority from the federal government to the states. President Nixon proposed several revenue-sharing measures to give the states greater financial control. President Reagan followed these measures with block grants to the states, designed to give states greater flexibility over the use of resources. As discussed earlier, the role of the federal government and its control over education is likely to decrease significantly during Trump's presidency.

However, President Bush's "No Child Left Behind," and President Obama's support of "Common Core" are two examples of the federal government expanding its influence and power. An additional example is the expansion of the role of the federal government with president Obama's signature legislation—"The Affordable Care Act," now commonly referred to as "Obamacare."

Funding for Special Needs

One basic tenet of American education is the concept of vertical equity. Because not all students have the same educational needs, funds must be provided to supplement the minimal amount allocated to each child. For example, children who score at a particularly low level on standardized tests are eligible for additional revenue. Special education children and the gifted and talented are also allotted additional funds in California.

Disagreements have arisen as to the amount of funding necessary for children with special needs. Some superintendents have argued that insufficient funds are allocated for special education students and that counties are skimming an inordinate amount of indirect cost off the top of district allotments.

Another group with special needs, students for whom English is a second language, is not a new concern. Indeed, heated discussion ensued as each wave of immigrants reached our shores. Educators at all levels have argued about the responsibility of public schools to accept newcomers and the language in which their education is best provided. This debate can be expected to continue for several generations.

Equal Opportunity

A typical third-grade teacher in California may have in his or her classroom several students with special needs. One pupil may be physically handicapped, while another requires additional reading instruction. Some students may have visited London and Paris, yet others have not traveled more than six blocks from home. The concept of equal opportunity plays an important role in these scenarios. Equal educational opportunity is based on the recognition that students have widely varying needs and abilities and the principle that school services should be linked to each student according to these characteristics. Additional or adaptive services should be available to students who need them. Compensatory education and special education services are well-known programs intended to ensure equality of educational opportunity.

Efficiency

The general public's desire for efficiency in the educational system is paralleled in the business community. Yet efficiency is extremely difficult to measure. Even within the profession, not to mention the communities our schools serve, we find disagreement on the actual product or outcome to be measured, concern over the ambiguous nature of "human output," confusion on the linkage of inputs to outcomes, and consequently, difficulty in determining cost-effectiveness.

School Finance Issues under Debate

Even though the responsible public agrees on the importance of education, disagreement abounds as to methods of taxation, alternative sources of income, and appropriate linkages between resources and students. Taxpayer revolts are a manifestation of disagreement on the best way to fund education.

In this section, major points of disagreement in school finance are discussed. Dilemmas to be addressed include:

- forms of taxation
- the voucher/choice/privatization issue
- the federal role in education
- the point of diminishing returns
- linkage of resources to outcomes
- alternative funding sources
- myths about money for schools.

Forms of Taxation

The choice of taxation that should support the educational system has been hotly debated. Most observers feel that a progressive tax system is most effective—one that increases the tax on individuals as their income rises. If the public determines that a tax is too heavy a burden, there follows a critical event such as the passage of Proposition 13, the tax revolt initiative in California in the late 1970s.

Characteristics of an ideal tax include production of consistent revenues, equity to those taxed, and ease of administration. Table 1 summarizes the major advantages and disadvantages of various taxes.

Even though the property tax was historically the major source of school revenues, it has not been without problems. Property assessment practices have been confusing, and the local aspect of the tax has been deemed unfair in some instances. The wide variation in tax-base wealth among local school districts is well documented in the literature.

The sales tax has been another means of obtaining revenue. It is easy to monitor and creates less public outcry than property taxes. However, the sales tax is classified as regressive because it sometimes collects most from those who can least afford to support the financial burden of public education.

The Voucher/Choice/Privatization Issue

In 2016 when Donald Trump was elected president, school choice and the voucher issue received nationwide attention. His Secretary of Education is a strong advocate for the two issues. But choice is not a new issue. Since the founding of the educational system, it has often been discussed and debated. In particular, the private and public sectors have been at odds over this question, which remains on the national agenda as the 21st century moves forward.

The voucher is a manifestation of school choice that involves issuance of a document entitling the student to schooling of family preference. As a proposition on the California ballot, the voucher initiative has not garnered enough public approval to pass, even though much effort has been expended in its behalf. An advantage advanced by voucher proponents is that the system gives families more influence over their children's education. This influence, they argue, would eventually generate market forces that would drive public schools to change for the better. One disadvantage, according to critics, is that the voucher would erode even further the low level of financial support for public education.

Table 1	Major Advantages and Disadvantages of Various Taxes	
Tax	**Advantages**	**Disadvantages**
Income Tax	Increase in amount in economically healthy periods Increases vertical equity	Decreases in amount in periods of economic slowdown Sometimes expensive to administer and monitor
Sales Tax	Inexpensive to implement Increases in amount in economically healthy periods	Regressive, i.e., becomes a burden on those least able to pay Decreases in amount in periods of economic slowdown
Property Tax	Usually consistent in periods of economic slowdown Ease of identifying the taxpayer	Perplexing equity issues Sometimes a burden for lower-income homeowners

The Federal Role in Education

There was little debate about the federal government's role in K–12 education until the second half of the 20th century. Prior to the 1950s, the U.S. Department of Health, Education, and Welfare exerted little influence over funding and management of education, which was regarded as a responsibility of the states. However, Congress and American citizens received a shock in 1957 when the Soviet Union launched Sputnik. This unexpected event resulted in passage and funding of the National Defense Education Act of 1958, legislation that provided federal support for education at all levels, from kindergarten to higher education.

Further expansion of the federal government's role in education took place under the leadership of President Lyndon Johnson. With Johnson's concept of "The Great Society," the school lunch program initiated under President Truman was expanded and a series of laws approved and funded to promote education. Funds were made available for a variety of programs, including those designed to improve achievement of educationally disadvantaged students. Head Start was promoted for preschool children, and funds were made available for school libraries. Then, under President Carter, a separate cabinet post was created for education, and the Office of Education became the U.S. Department of Education.

During most of the first half of the 20th century, support for federal intervention in education was divided along party lines, with Republicans generally opposing federal education programs and Democrats supporting the concept. The disagreement reached its zenith with the election of President Reagan, who threatened to abolish the Department of Education.

However, the early 1990s saw a major shift of educational policy in the Republican Party when President George Bush supported America 2000, originally developed by the governors of the 50 states. Since President Bill Clinton had led the development of those six goals, it is not surprising that—with two additions—he endorsed the same program, renamed Goals 2000, when he took office. No further mention was made of abolishing the Department of Education. In the election of 2000, when Al Gore faced off against George W. Bush, both Democrats and Republicans embraced support for education. This support continued in 2004 with Bush defeating Kerry.

Bush listed education as his number one priority, dramatized by the slogan: "No child shall be left behind." This legislation and the Bush presidency saw the greatest increase in funding and control of education in the nation's history.

President Obama, elected in 2008 and re-elected in 2012, largely embraced the tenets of "No Child Left Behind," but placed a greater focus on rewarding high achieving teachers, schools, and districts. As discussed earlier, President Trump largely campaigned on returning educational decisions to the states and local communities. This battle over the federal role in education will likely continue over the next several years.

The Point of Diminishing Returns

One classic question is fascinating to discuss: What is the point beyond which additional expenditures yield little or no increased educational returns? This issue can realistically be called the "mystery spot" of public education. The point is theoretical, since there is no precise agreement on educational outcomes. Nevertheless, it is assumed that most educational systems in the United States are at a point far below any risk of no return simply because financial support for education has eroded in recent years.

Nevertheless, this issue has been a popular topic of research papers for decades. During 2016-2017 Idaho spent $6,538 per pupil, the least amount on education, while Vermont spent the greatest amount at $23,557. The national average was $11,787. California was 22nd at $11,330 per student (NEA, 2017).

Did Vermont's spending result in greater student achievement than Idaho? According to the National Center for Education Statistics (2015), the answer is "yes," but not by very much. Idaho's grade four reading score was 222, while Vermont's was 230. Fourth grade math scores in Idaho were 239, while Vermont students scored 243.

Linking Expenditures to Student Outcomes

The concept of "educational productivity" is gaining ground. The belief that schools need to increase student achievement and that achievement is directly related to expenditures has become widespread across the nation. Indeed, a series of "adequacy lawsuits" is forcing states—including New York and other high-expenditure states—to increase the amount of money spent on schools. Nevertheless, Alfred Lindseth, a private attorney practicing education law, argues that these lawsuits are misguided in that they will focus the debate on money rather than on programs and will shift control of education still further to state, rather than local, government (Lindseth, 2004).

Allocating financial resources to education is a responsibility of federal, state, and local lawmakers. However, procedures for determining these allocations have been ambiguous, subject to varied interpretations. At times, governmental bodies have distributed resources based upon political expediency. In such an environment, education may be at a disadvantage because of the difficulty of measuring increased output as a consequence of additional input.

Policymakers must decide what aspects of student achievement are the school's responsibility and what factors, such as student poverty, are beyond the school's control or outside the school's responsibility. As a result of this emphasis on accountability, educators are coming to realize that they must be attentive to all their clients, including parents, community members, and individual politicians.

Alternative Funding Sources

A potentially exciting area of study is that of alternative funding sources. These are sources that have typically not been tapped in the past. Many have caused a flood of controversy, even though, like the "use tax," they have not been applied to any great extent.

Site-Value Tax

This is a tax on the actual value of land, even though it may be unimproved. As the value of the land appreciates, the tax increases. Other countries use this system with good results.

Value-Added Tax

In its clearest form, VAT is a tax on the value of goods at each transaction level, from production to consumption. The tax can be levied on each good or service at each stage.

Lottery

In 2014, lotteries were run in 44 states plus the District of Columbia, Puerto Rico, and the U.S. Virgin Islands (Wikipedia, 2014). Their popularity probably lies in the low price of the tickets coupled with the hope that one might become wealthy. Studies have shown that most purchasers of lottery tickets are either poor or middle class.

In California, 34 cents out of every lottery dollar is allocated to education. This sounds like a large proportion; however, the lottery has not provided the windfall for education that some expected. Lottery monies typically constitute only 1% to 2% of a school district's revenue. In addition, school officials at the state level sometimes draw on lottery income to supplement state allotments.

Private Foundations

The private sector is proving a fertile ground for development of new revenue sources. Private foundations established in connection with a school district have met with mixed results. Their success depends to a great extent upon the wealth of community members, although motivated educators have sparked community giving in some districts that receive less funding from the state.

School-Business Partnerships

Partnerships between schools and businesses are not completely altruistic, as both sides typically benefit. However, both partners seek the same goal—to prepare students for the 21st century. In the most successful partnerships, a business works directly with the school it is supporting. Many schools report success with businesses operating within a five-mile radius. An example of a creative partnership is that of a Los Angeles high school class that succeeded at selling salad dressing, made as part of a class project, in local grocery stores.

Myths about Money for Schools

Two hotly debated myths about money and schooling have clouded public discussion of finance for schools. The first of these is that the United States spends more money on its schools than any other nation in the world. This myth was widely disseminated during the George Bush administration. The second myth is that money makes no difference in student achievement. These two myths are so prevalent that they are quoted from backyard fences to the corridors of Congress.

The Organization for Economic Cooperation and Development (OECD, 2013) reports that the United States is 5th of 34 nations in education spending as a percentage of GDP (gross domestic product). The top four nations include Iceland, Korea, Israel, and Norway.

The second myth, that there is no relationship between money and achievement, is not supported by the evidence. The Huffington Post (2013) reports that the states that spend the most on education get the best results. The top-spending states are in the top 15 in fourth and eighth grades math and reading proficiency examinations. Among the 10 states that spent the least per pupil, only Colorado was in the top 10 on the proficiency tests.

High school graduation rates are also likely to be higher in the states that spend more per student. Students are also more likely to complete college. More than 30% of adults in the top-spending states had at least a bachelor's degree, compared to the U.S. rate of 28.5%. Of the 10 states that spent the least per student, 8 had below-average percentages with bachelor's degrees (The Huffington Post, 2013).

Is it true that expenditures are unrelated to pupil achievement? As discussed earlier with the examples in Vermont and Idaho, the money spent per student does make a difference, but not proportionately.

Looking Ahead

Four tenets set a foundation for future directions in school finance:

1. The cost of education will continue to escalate. If California persists in placing education near the bottom of its funding priorities, the mismatch between rising costs and low student achievement will create an unresolvable dilemma.
2. The economic and cultural conditions of students will continue to affect their educational attainment. This relationship will impact the funding required to bring all students to a "level playing field."
3. Differences among students in ability, interest, and the desire to attain graduation will continue to complicate the process of allocating resources to education.
4. There is no disagreement concerning the economic and non-economic benefits of education. Educational attainment is tied to future earnings, and non-economic benefits are considerable.

State priorities will impact the first point to a great degree. If California experiences an economic downturn in any given year, this decline directly affects funds allocated to students. Since the tenth amendment determines that education is a state responsibility, the actions of the legislature must be monitored closely.

Secondly, the economic and cultural milieu of students has a powerful impact on their educational attainment. The California Public Policy Institute conducts an annual survey of California children (Bohn, 2017). The key findings of the 2017 survey reveal:

1. California ranks low compared to other states in the percentage of personal income spent on education.
2. Almost one out of five (19.9%) California children live at the poverty level.
3. The poverty rate for Latino children (29.6%) was more than double that of Asian-American children (14.4%), and white children (11.5%).

The third issue, differential ability among students, affects the quantity of resources necessary to educate them. Attempts will continue to be made to assign more resources to underachieving schools in the hope of giving their pupils an opportunity to graduate from high school. Differential resources will also continue to be necessary for students with special physical needs and language requirements. Another debatable issue: How much should the federal government subsidize these costs?

There are no arguments regarding the fourth point—that education brings both economic and non-economic benefits. Each added year of education can be tied to a higher average future earnings figure that is difficult to dispute. Consequently, opponents to revenue increases need to consider the long-term costs when education is *not* provided. It is interesting to note that with few exceptions, states with the lowest dropout rate also have the lowest rate of prisoners per 100,000 people. Where, then, should monies be invested: in prisons, welfare plans, law enforcement—or education?

An optimistic observation with implications for the future of education is that most parents of school-age children are happy with their neighborhood school. They realize that, expensive as public education may be, the cost to society of not educating its people is far higher. The detrimental societal effect of illiteracy, welfare, and prison occupancy is untenable in the long term. Considering the lifelong return in earnings and the large investment already made, California must provide the best education for its youth, regardless of their place of residence, the affluence of their parents, or the economic wealth of the school district.

SUMMARY

Most American citizens support public education. Since the end of the cold war, and despite the national focus on the war against terrorism, education has become the top or near top priority. Despite a general consensus that education needs to be reformed and improved, however, the meaning of "reformed" and "improved" is unclear. Older citizens yearn for the "good old days," with an emphasis on citizenship and the "three Rs," while others expound on "thinking outside the box." Managers of national and international enterprises bemoan the lack of skills among employees, while artists and musicians decry the lack of culture in the schools.

Educational debate reached a zenith at the national level in the presidential campaign of 2000 between Al Gore and George W. Bush, with each candidate promising to be "The Education President." Debate centered around a number of issues, including school choice, national assessment, and the level of federal financial support for education. It is predicted that education will continue as a major priority of American citizens well into the 21st century, with ongoing debate on the goals of education and its financial support.

KEY TERMS

Alternative funding

Diminishing return

Equity and efficiency

Fiscal federalism

Income tax

Local autonomy

Private and public good of education

Private foundation

Property tax

Sales tax

School-business partnerships

Site-value tax

Special needs

Value-added tax (VAT)

Voucher/choice/privatization

1. Discuss three major arguments in support of "the public good of education."

2. Equity and efficiency are desirable goals of American public education. Briefly define each term. Discuss the goal you feel is most achievable. Explain your answer.

3. Schools are supported by several sources of tax dollars. Which of the modes of taxation do you feel is most advantageous for supporting public education? Why?

4. "Choice" continues to be hotly debated in the 21st century. What are the advantages and disadvantages of providing parents with a choice of public school? private school?

History of California School Finance

Introduction

The story of formal education in California begins with the Franciscan missions. For pupils other than Indians, 55 schools were established during the Spanish and Mexican periods. All were elementary schools, and most of them functioned only briefly. On April 3, 1848, San Francisco established the first California public school, taught by Thomas Douglas. Two months later, four of the five trustees, several students, and schoolmaster Douglas abandoned the school and left for the goldfields (Caughey, 1943).

With growing population and California statehood in 1850, the demand for public schools accelerated. Reflecting this demand, the first state constitution required the legislature to provide for a school in each district in the state. However, the school was only required to operate three months per year. San Francisco again took the lead and opened its first public high school in 1856. Between 1850 and the early 1900s, as California's population expanded, the number of public schools increased (Caughey, 1943).

During the second half of the 20th century and first decade of the 21st century, California school districts and communities struggled to provide facilities, equipment, and staff for public schools. This struggle was often taken out of the control of school boards and citizens in the local districts. Rather, the state legislature and the courts played a dominant role in control and finance of public education. In addition, citizens of California have often relied on the initiative process to provide direction to school curriculum and funding. This chapter highlights those major court cases, propositions, legislation, and events that have influenced public education in California.

Student Population

As the richest state in the West, California could afford to finance public schools. As of 1940, the state's per capita expenditure was exceeded only by that of New York. Nevertheless, California experienced ongoing difficulties in providing adequate financing for public education. The situation was exacerbated by the rapid increase in school population, which more than doubled between 1914 and 1940.

With the coming of World War II, California school districts were again overwhelmed by a tremendous increase in population. School districts in the vicinity of war plants and military bases were confronted with a sudden increase in enrollment, far beyond any expectations. To cope with increased enrollment, some districts constructed completely new schools. Other districts, however, had to rely on crowding more students into existing buildings, often forcing schools and teachers to do double duty through half-day sessions.

One of every eight school children in the United States were enrolled in California schools. In 2016 California's K-12 public school enrollment of 6,226,814 was the largest of any state. The second largest school enrollment was that of Texas, two-thirds the size of California, with an estimated enrollment of 5,289,235. To illustrate how large that is, more students are enrolled in California's public schools than the combined total populations in Alaska, Delaware, Idaho, North Dakota, South Dakota, Montana, Vermont, and Wyoming (NEA, 2017).

Second Half of the 20th Century & Early 21st Century

During the second half of the 20th century, a series of court decisions, propositions, and legislation resulted in a shift from property taxes to other forms of taxation as the primary source of funds for education in California. This change resulted, to a significant degree, in transferring local control of education to state control. With this change, school finance became much more complex.

Public education has also been greatly influenced by California's governors and the priority each has placed on education. As the 20th century drew to a close, Governors Pete Wilson and Gray Davis both ran on platforms supporting public education. Davis, elected in 1998, introduced a series of educational reforms that greatly impacted education. Governor Schwarzenegger replaced Governor Davis in the recall election of 2003, pledging strong support for public education.

In 2010, Jerry Brown was elected as governor for his third term. He had previously served two terms from 1976 to 1983. He pledged support for education and strongly supported Proposition 30, which provided financial support for schools and colleges. This proposition is discussed in more detail later in this chapter.

This chapter provides a historical perspective by discussing major legal actions affecting education, including the court decision in *Serrano v. Priest*, Senate Bill 90, Proposition 13, the Gann Limit, Senate Bill 813, Proposition 37, Proposition 98, Proposition 111, Senate Bills 1977 and 376, and Propositions 227, 38, 39, and 49.

1968—*Serrano v. Priest*

Prior to 1972, school district finances were largely dependent upon property taxes, which furnished about 2/3 of education revenues during those years. Since these taxes were determined by the city or other legal entity in which the taxpayer lived, per-pupil resources for education varied widely. Reliance on local property taxes as a major source of school revenues inevitably produces fiscal inequities because the property tax base is not distributed equally across school districts.

As a result, property-poor districts usually have low resources and expenditures per pupil, even when they levy a high tax rate. By the same token, property-rich districts usually enjoy high resources and expenditures per pupil, even with a low tax rate. At the time the *Serrano* suit was brought to court, educational expenditures per student ranged from $274 in one California district to $1,710 in another, a ratio of more than 6:1.

In 1968 a group of attorneys brought suit in the California courts in behalf of John Serrano against Ivy Baker Priest, who was California's State Treasurer at that time. John Serrano was a student enrolled in Baldwin Park School District, a low-revenue district. At that time, Baldwin Park was spending $577 per student, while the Beverly Hills school district was spending $1,223. This inequity was due to the difference in assessed valuation of property per pupil in the two districts: $50,885 in Beverly Hills and $3,706 in Baldwin Park, a ratio of nearly 14:1.

The school tax rate paid in the two districts revealed a reverse inequity: Baldwin Park taxpayers were paying $5.48 per $100 of assessed valuation while Beverly Hills residents paid only $2.38 per $100. Attorneys for Serrano argued that the 14th Amendment to the U.S. Constitution and the Education Clause of the California Constitution made it unconstitutional for school revenues per pupil to be linked to local property wealth.

The California Supreme Court decided the case in favor of the plaintiff. In upholding the *Serrano* decision, the California Supreme Court held that the state tax system violated the right of students to receive an equal education. *Serrano* was followed by cases in 45 other states that claimed state funding was unconstitutional. Of these, 25 upheld the challenge. Only five states have never had a lawsuit: Delaware, Hawaii, Mississippi, Nevada, and Utah (Access quality education, 2012).

1972—Senate Bill 90

In 1972 the State of California enacted Senate Bill 90 (SB 90), which limited the maximum amount of general purpose state and local revenues a local district could receive. The revenue limit formula set a base amount per student, added an adjustment for students with special needs, and further increased the limit in response to inflation. The key equalization feature was an adjustment that provided a higher dollar amount to low-revenue districts. As SB 90 was implemented, high-revenue districts found their revenue limits leveling down toward a statewide average.

Yet in 1974, a California Superior Court ruled that progress toward equalization was too little and too slow. The court decreed that disparities must decrease at a faster rate. Finally, 15 years later, in 1989, the California Appellate Court ruled that satisfactory progress had been made, and the case was closed.

1977—Assembly Bill 65

The California Assembly approved Assembly Bill 65 in 1977. This legislation was written in response to the *Serrano v. Priest* decision. In an attempt to equalize revenue limits among California school districts, it created an annual inflation adjustment based on a sliding scale. Higher cost-of-living increases were to go to districts with low revenue limits, while higher revenue districts would receive a smaller increase. This adjustment became known as the "squeeze factor."

1978—Proposition 13

When voters approved Proposition 13, also known as the Jarvis Amendment, they created massive changes in school funding in California. The leaders of this tax revolt, Howard Jarvis and Paul Gann, dramatically changed the system of taxation in this state and, eventually, nationwide. The two men were an odd couple who shared a vision of lower property taxes. Jarvis had been publisher of a small newspaper in Utah; in the early 1960s he moved to Southern California, where he became a political anti-tax crusader. Gann, a preacher's son, quoted Biblical passages in a soothing drawl that was reminiscent of his Arkansas roots.

With successful passage of Proposition 13, Howard Jarvis became a celebrity. He appeared on talk shows, his picture was featured on the cover of *Time* magazine, and his success resulted in Proposition 13-type tax revolts in other parts of the country.

The problem of ever-increasing property taxes in California had been real. The 1960s and 1970s were a time of escalating inflation in California, particularly acute in the cost of homes. One of the authors of this text purchased a home in 1964 for $23,000 and saw the price double within a three-year period, along with a like increase in the assessed value and property tax. Some retirees could not afford their property tax bills and faced the prospect of having to sell homes they had purchased after World War II.

However, although Proposition 13 rolled back property taxes, it had unintended consequences. It did much more than change California's property tax system. California politics would never be the same. Today, almost all California tax dollars flow to Sacramento, where the state takes its cut, then sends what is left back to school districts, counties, and cities. But that is not all. The state legislature, much like an autocratic father, not only distributes the money, but also decrees how it will be spent. The most dramatic and far-reaching effect of Proposition 13 was to shift power in education from local school districts and municipalities to Sacramento.

Proposition 13 resulted in a generation of leaders dead set against raising taxes, and it was a boon for homeowners and businesses. The initiative immediately cut taxes by more than 50%, or $6.1 billion, statewide. This tax revolt persevered as an American way of life long after the two tax crusaders left the scene. Politically, cutting taxes has been popular in state and national battles for Congress and the White House. Some political analysts attribute a major cause of President George Bush's defeat in 1992 to his famous "Read my lips: no new taxes" statement—a promise that, as it turned out, he was unable to keep.

Proposition 13 imposed a 1% limit on general purpose property tax rates, calculated either on the 1975–76 value of the property plus a maximum 2% annual inflation increase—or on the purchase price upon sale. When a district computes its revenue limit, it may find its share of the 1% to be higher or lower than its calculated revenue limit. If there is a shortfall, the state allocates funds to ensure that the district receives its per-pupil revenue limit.

A growing concern in consequence of Proposition 13 focuses on the unequal collection of taxes on similar, neighboring properties. A property that is sold becomes taxable on its selling price, thus generating a higher tax bill than one subject only to the 2% annual increase. Earlier, the California Supreme Court had refused to hear three cases on the subject.

However, in the spring of 1991 the U.S. Supreme Court accepted a lawsuit by Macy's department store. That suit was withdrawn by Macy's, but the court agreed to decide a similar suit brought by a Los Angeles homeowner (*Nordlinger v. Hahn*, Case No. 90-1912). The plaintiff, Stephanie Nordlinger, argued that Proposition 13 violated equal protection under the law, as stipulated in the 14th amendment to the federal constitution. Ms. Nordlinger, who purchased a house in 1988 for $170,000, was paying about $1,700 a year in property taxes. Nordlinger's neighbors, who had owned similar houses before Proposition 13 went into effect, paid $350 to $400 per year.

In June 1992 the U.S. Supreme Court ruled that Proposition 13 was legal. Although the ruling called the property tax system distasteful and unwise, the court refused to upset the will of the people of California as expressed in Proposition 13. In an eight-to-one ruling, the court said Proposition 13 does not violate the U.S. Constitutional guarantee of equal protection under the law, even though it grants tax relief to longtime residents at the expense of new homeowners. Justice Harry A. Blackburn, writing for the court, said, "The states have a large leeway in making classifications for tax purposes as long as they do not discriminate against a particular group, such as blacks or women" (Savage, 1992).

The major impact of Proposition 13 has been a higher level of state aid. As a result, K–12 education has become almost totally dependent upon fluctuations in the state economy, instead of the more reliable property tax. Anything that has a negative impact on state revenues, such as the earthquakes in San Francisco, Landers, and San Fernando or the enormous cost of electrical energy in response to the shortage of 2001, has negative impact on the state's ability to fund education.

1979—Gann Limit

As part of the "taxpayers' revolt" in the late 70s, the Gann limit was approved in November of 1979 in the form of Proposition 4. This constitutional amendment established limits on allowable growth in state and local government spending. The limits permit government spending to increase at a rate no faster than inflation and the change in population. The result of this amendment was to make state spending an ever-decreasing percentage of personal income. The Gann limit created a "squeeze" on resources available to local school districts in addition to that previously generated by Proposition 13. The Gann Limit's power has eroded over the years by other education initiatives and was virtually toothless by the start of the 21st century.

1983—Senate Bill 813

School funding improved in 1983–84. This improvement resulted in part from the fact that the 1982–83 recession was of short duration, so that the state economy grew strongly in 1983–84. The second reason for improvement was that educators, parents, and business leaders formed a coalition that accomplished passage of SB 813, known as the Hughes/Hart Education Reform Act.

This bill marked the first step after *Serrano* toward rehabilitation of education in California. Programs were implemented to increase the length of the school year and the school day, the mentor teacher program was instituted, and beginning teachers' salaries were improved. Other reforms included mini-grants for teachers, funding for instructional materials, and increased counseling for high school sophomores. However, even with these changes, California still ranked below the national average in per-pupil expenditures for education.

1984—Proposition 37: California State Lottery

The California State Lottery Act (Proposition 37) was approved by the voters in 1984 and implemented by the state legislature in 1985. The Lottery Act states that the purpose of the California lottery is to generate funding to supplement the public education budget to the extent of at least 34% of sales. In the year 2000, Proposition 20 was approved by the people of California. This proposition requires that one-half of any growth in lottery money be used to purchase instructional materials.

1988—Proposition 98

Proposition 98 was approved by voters in November of 1988—again as a result of joint effort by parents and educators, including the California Teachers' Association. This proposition established a constitutionally-based, minimum funding floor for K–14 education. Proposition 98 retains education's first right to state revenues. Proposition 98 includes the following provisions:

- maintenance of a sufficient reserve by the state
- adoption of a "School Accountability Report Card," which details student achievement, dropout rate, class size, and similar items
- a formula that adjusts revenue allocations beyond the Gann limitations
- minimum base funding (40.33% of tax revenue) for K–14 education.

Proposition 98, as subsequently modified by Proposition 111 (see next section), contains three tests to determine minimum base funding for public schools:

- **Test 1** requires the state to allocate to K–14 school districts at least 34.55% of state general fund taxes. This is equal to the percentage set in 1986–87, but adjusted for the property tax shift to K–14 districts.
- **Test 2** requires that districts receive at least the same amount of state aid and local tax dollars as in the prior year, plus statewide K–12 ADA growth and an inflation factor equal to the annual percentage change in per capita personal income.
- **Test 3** was added with the passage of Proposition 111 in 1990. It states that when growth in state taxes per capita plus 1/2% is less than growth in California personal income per capita, then the Test 2 inflation factor is reduced to growth in state taxes per capita plus 1/2%.

The effect of these tests depends on state revenues, local property taxes, enrollment growth, personal income, and state population. Proposition 98 minimum funding level is generally calculated under Test 2, which is unrelated to current economic factors. However, in very good economic years, Test 1 applies, while in a very bad economic period, such as the recession years in the early 1990s, Test 3 applies. The proposition also includes a provision that allows the state to suspend base funding provisions for one year by enacting urgency legislation. Such a suspension requires a 2/3 vote in both houses of the legislature and the signature of the governor.

1990—Proposition 111

Proposition 111 was approved by California voters in June of 1990. Although this proposition was called "The Traffic Congestion Relief and Spending Limitation Act of 1990," popularly referred to as the "gas tax," it contained several provisions regarding funds for education. In addition to continuing to provide public education and community colleges with at least 40% of the state general fund budget, Proposition 111 also revised the formula for the minimum funding guarantee for public schools and community colleges.

As described above, Proposition 98 guaranteed, first, the "1986–87 percentage of revenues formula," giving schools and colleges collectively the same percentage of state general fund tax revenues as received in 1986–87. Also included is the second, now called "maintenance of effort," guarantee. This section assures to schools and colleges their prior year funding level, adjusted for increases in enrollment and adjustments in cost of living (COLA). Proposition 111 changed the cost-of-living basis in the "maintenance of effort" formula. Specifically, it requires that per capita personal income in California, rather than the lower U.S. Consumer Price Index, serve as the COLA to determine maintenance of effort.

The proposition also allows the state to reduce the minimum funding guarantee in a year of low revenue growth. However, should that provision be activated, the funding base must be restored in subsequent years so education eventually receives the amount that would have been allocated had no reduction occurred.

The impact of this measure depends upon its effect on the minimum funding guarantee and on excess revenues. Generally speaking, Proposition 111 tends to increase the minimum funding guarantee because it increases the cost-of-living element in the maintenance of effort formula. Thus, the maintenance of effort formula more often determines the amount of the guarantee.

1991—Assembly Bill 1200: School District Accountability

Assembly Bill 1200 requires school districts to track and report their revenues and expenditures each year. The law requires districts to project their fiscal solvency two years out and provide the state with financial reports twice a year. County Offices of Education are responsible for monitoring and providing technical assistance to districts within the county. Additional information on this requirement is contained in chapter five.

1996—Senate Bill 1777: Class Size Reduction

With the downturn in California's economy during the late 1980s and early 1990s, schools received nothing, or very little, by way of a cost-of-living adjustment (COLA). As a result, districts balanced their budgets by increasing class size. The ratio of California students per teacher (including reading specialists and others with out-of-classroom assignments) increased K–12 from 27:1 in 1995 to 29:1 in 1997. The state had the second largest student:teacher ratio in the U.S. until 1996–97, when Governor Wilson and the California Legislature approved funds to lower class size in K–3 grades to a maximum of 20 students per teacher (Children's Advocacy Institute, 2001).

Within two years, the student:teacher ratio in the primary grades approached the national level. However, classes in grades 4–12 continued to exceed the national average. EdSource estimated that in 2001–02 California had risen only to 48th among the 50 states in number of students per teacher. Although the California average fell to 20.8 students per teacher, the national average had meanwhile improved even more—to 15.9 (EdSource, 2003a).

Over the next several years, California's student–teacher ratio continued to be one of the highest in the nation. The National Education Association (2017) reported that California had the fourth highest number of students per teacher with 22.5 students per teacher. The national average was 15.9.

California's Governor Brown signed a new law in 2013 that established new goals for class size reduction. The new funding formula gives school districts additional funds if they can keep the average class size for kindergarten through third grade to 24 students. To receive full funding, districts will have eight years to get their class size in K-3 reduced to an average of 24 (Mongeau, 2013).

1997—Senate Bill 1468: Average Daily Attendance Accounting

This legislation changed how Average Daily Attendance (ADA) is counted. Before 1997, ADA equaled the number of students in school plus those students who missed school, but had a permissible excuse such as illness, doctor's appointment, or a death in the family. Now, schools calculate ADA by counting only the students who are actually at school each day. To offset the loss of revenue, the state provided a higher per pupil revenue for each ADA.

1997—Senate Bill 376: Standardized Testing and Reporting (STAR) Program

Under the leadership of Governor Pete Wilson, the Standardized Testing and Reporting (STAR) program was approved by the legislature in 1997. This legislation requires all California school districts to use a single standardized test to assess each student in grades two through eleven each year. The California Board of Education selected the Stanford Achievement Test, Ninth Edition (SAT9) as the test to be administered. Subsequently, SAT9 was replaced by the California Achievement Test, Sixth Edition (CAT6).

The STAR program almost made it to 30 years. It was replaced with the California Assessment of Student Performance and Progress (CAASPP) in 2013. The new test is Smarter Balanced Assessment exam (SBAC), which is discussed in more detail later in this chapter. Students started taking the new assessment in 2014.

The objective of the testing program is to provide California citizens, the legislature, and educators with an objective view of student achievement.

1998—Proposition 227: Bilingual Education

The original objective of bilingual education was to ensure that students would not fall behind academically because of a poor command of English and that students would gradually be taught English as a second language. Those who favored this approach argued that if language-minority students were taught some subjects in their native tongue, they would learn English without sacrificing content knowledge.

This proposition was overwhelmingly approved, and it virtually eliminated California's bilingual program. The proposition required that limited English proficient (LEP) students be placed in English immersion classes and later mainstreamed into regular classes.

The debate over how best to instruct linguistically diverse students continued. In 2016 the terms of Proposition 227 were overturned with the passage of a new law. Proposition 58 is discussed later in this chapter.

1999—Assembly Bill 1600: Charter Schools Funding

This legislation gives charter schools the option of receiving funding directly from the state, instead of through their local school district. The funds come as a block grant. This revenue combines general-purpose money and a portion of categorical funds into a single per-pupil amount. This legislation contributed to the growth of charter schools as it simplified distribution of funds to charter schools.

1998–2003—Governor Davis

Governor Davis ran on a campaign of strong support for schools. In his first State of the State address in January 1999, Davis made it clear that education would be his "first, second, and third priority" (Davis, 1999). Under his legislation, he continued to fund the class size program initiated by Governor Wilson and expanded the program by providing funds to reduce class size in the 9th grade as well. Other initiatives included the Teacher Peer Assistance and Review Program (PAR), and Public Schools Accountability Act, which approved a mandatory high school exit examination. Each of these programs is briefly discussed.

1999—Morgan-Hart Class Size Reduction

This act provides funds to school districts that reduce class size in ninth grade English and one other 9th grade subject required for graduation. The other course may include mathematics, science, or social studies. Average class size is limited to 20 students per teacher and no more than 22 in any participating class. Funds for this program were included in the categorical flexibility budget in 2007 and are no longer provided.

1999—Teacher Peer Assistance and Review Program (PAR)

Governor Davis allocated funds to districts to implement the Teacher Peer Assistance and Review Program (PAR). The program is designed to improve the performance of veteran teachers. PAR requires teachers, administrators, districts, and unions to work together to assist veteran teachers in improving their instructional programs.

Unfortunately, funding for this program was cut sharply in 2002–03 and again during the next several years. Prior to 2008–09, funds for this program were restricted; they could only be used for the PAR program. After 2008–09, the funds were unrestricted; they can be used for other programs. Therefore, the future of the program is uncertain.

1999—High School Proficiency Examination

In 1999 Governor Davis proposed, and the legislature approved, a mandatory high school exit examination. The examination is to look at the academic areas of language arts and math. The original plan was that, beginning in 2004, high school students would not graduate if they could not pass the examination, which is meant to certify that all graduates possess the skills and knowledge needed to be successful in college or the workplace.

California students took the exam from 2003-2004 through 2012-2013. After that date it was no longer required. In the last year of the test, 85% of students passed the math test, and 83% passed the English test on their first try.

2000—Proposition 20: Cardenas Textbook Act of 2000

Citizens of California modified the Lottery Act in 2000 with a mandate that 50% of any increase in lottery funds could only be spent for instructional materials. Starting with the 1998–99 fiscal year, districts received an unrestricted lottery amount and a restricted amount, which could only be spent for instructional materials. The restricted amount has averaged between $19.00 and $41.00 over the past several years.

2000—Proposition 38: Schools of Choice (The Voucher Initiative)

The notion of allowing parents to choose a school for their children to attend was part of President George Bush's educational program and was supported by California Governor Pete Wilson. In 1992 proponents circulated an initiative entitled "Parent Choice" that would have required California to provide a scholarship or voucher for every school-age child in an amount equal to at least 50% of state and local funding for K–12 education.

The initiative, Proposition 174, received enough signatures to appear on the June 1994 ballot. However, Governor Wilson placed the initiative on the ballot for November 1993. The initiative was overwhelmingly defeated by nearly 70% of those who went to the polls. At that time, supporters of the voucher vowed to continue the fight for "schools of choice," announcing that another initiative could be expected in the future.

The future took seven years to arrive. Proposition 38, another voucher initiative, was placed on the November 2000 ballot. This proposition was sponsored by Tim Draper, a Silicon Valley millionaire. The proposition echoed Proposition 174 with the exception that the voucher would carry a value of $4,000, instead of the $2,600 offered in 1993. Draper hoped to avoid some of the criticism of Proposition 174 by writing in a requirement that any private school that accepted a voucher had to conduct academic testing.

The education community breathed a huge sigh of relief when the measure failed with a 71% "no" vote. Time will tell whether the voucher movement is dead in California or will be revived for a third time.

2000—Proposition 39: General Obligation Bonds

Although local General Obligation (GO) Bond elections were eliminated by Proposition 13, they were reinstated in 1986 by passage of Proposition 46. This proposition was an important restoration of capital outlay funding ability to school districts. It also allowed school districts to form special districts to sell construction bonds, subject to 2/3 approval of the voters in the special district.

The catch for many California districts was the 2/3 requirement. Most districts discovered that in the face of strong local resistance, passage of a bond initiative was next to impossible.

Consequently, the educational community attempted several times to change the requirement for passage of a GO bond measure from 2/3 of the vote to a simple majority. California citizens voted on this change in majority requirement in 1993 and the spring of 2000. Both measures failed. As a compromise, the educational community agreed to place Proposition 39 on the fall 2000 ballot. This proposition, which passed by a narrow margin, lowered the required vote for passage of general obligation bonds from 2/3 to 55%. More details regarding bond issues and requirements are discussed in Chapter 15, the facilities chapter.

2002—Proposition 49: After-School Education and Safety

Proposition 49, which in 2002 created the After-School Education and Safety Program, provides funds for a variety of after-school programs. Arnold Schwarzenegger, prior to his election as California's governor, was a major sponsor of this initiative. Supporters of the program made the argument that the program would save money by reducing costs for corrections and remedial education.

Funds are available to elementary schools, middle schools, and junior high schools. Districts are encouraged to establish programs that provide tutoring and enrichment activities in kindergarten through grade 9 outside the regular school day. The state is not obligated to provide funds for all students who wish to participate in the program. The annual level of funding is determined through the budget process and schools must apply for the funds. Schools whose enrollment is made up predominantly of low-income students are given priority for funding.

2003–2010—Election of Schwarzenegger

Arnold Schwarzenegger first gained fame as a bodybuilder when he won the Mr. Universe title at age 20 and won the title of Mr. Olympia seven times. His fame continued as an action movie star in a variety of films including "The Terminator," "Batman and Robin," and "True Lies."

His entry into politics was the sponsorship of Proposition 49, the ballot initiative that established after-school programs (discussed earlier). This success led to speculation that he would run for governor in 2006. However, the opportunity came earlier in 2003 with the recall of Governor Davis.

There were two questions on the special election ballot of 2003. The first question was should Governor Davis be recalled? This question was approved by 55 percent of California voters. The second question was who should replace Governor Davis. Arnold Schwarzenegger was elected governor with a 49 percent vote to complete Davis' term of office.

Schwarzenegger campaigned on the promise of "action, action, action," and on his first day in office signed an executive order repealing an unpopular car tax that added $4 billion to the $10 billion gap between state spending and revenues. He ended his first year as governor with a 60 percent voter approval rating, but his ratings had dropped with teachers and other public employee unions.

In 2005, Governor Schwarzenegger took the education community by surprise in his January "State of the State" speech by proposing merit pay for teachers. Moreover, he proposed increasing the length of teaching experience from two years to five for teachers to acquire tenure (DiMassa & Rubin, 2005).

As expected, the teacher unions did not accept the proposal warmly. DiMassa and Rubin (2005) quoted Terry Presta, president of the San Diego Education Association, "It's a crazy idea . . . just another blast at teachers" (p. A5). The unions were successful in keeping the merit pay plan from the ballot and the California electorate soundly defeated the tenure proposals.

2010—Senate Bill X5.1—Common Core Standards

Teachers and educational leaders have argued for decades that the nation's students need to improve academic achievement in order to compete with the rest of the world. To improve student achievement, each state adopted state standards for grade levels and subjects. California adopted state standards in 1998.

The California School Board approved the Common Core Standards in 2010, and implementation has continued during the past several years. New curriculum and standards in English and math have progressed at a rapid rate in most of the state.

Governor Brown and the state legislature have demonstrated support for Common Core. Brown included funds in the state budget for school districts to provide professional development, technology, and the purchase of instructional materials. Additional information on this topic is presented in Chapter 3.

2012—Proposition 30—Temporary Tax to Fund Education

In 2012, after five years of economic decline, government retrenchment, and widespread loss of confidence in the future, California began showing the first signs of rebound. One of the major reasons for change was voter approval of Proposition 30.

Proposition 30, called the Temporary Tax to Fund Education, was approved by California voters by 55%. Governor Brown provided strong leadership in the passage of this proposition. Proposition 30 raised California's sales tax to 7.5% from 7.25%. The sales tax increase went into effect in 2013 and ended in 2016.

This proposition increased the income tax for those earning over $250,000 per year. The money from Proposition 30 stabilized school funding, and made it possible for school districts to live within their budgets. This funding avoided the dismissal of thousands of teachers, which had become a yearly practice in many districts. The state legislature was able to balance the budget for the first time in several years without cutting school funding and other programs.

The tax was scheduled to end in 2021, but a new proposition, which is discussed later, extended the tax to 2030. The income from the tax increase is primarily allocated to K-12 schools and colleges.

2013—ASSEMBLY BILL 484: California Assessment of Student Performance and Progress (CAASPP)

CAASPP replaces the Standardized Testing and Reporting (STAR) Program. The primary goal of the assessment system is to assist teachers, administrators, students, and parents by promoting high-quality teaching and learning.

The assessment is called Smarter Balanced. The tests used in the STAR program were multiple choice, except for writing assessments in grades 4 and 7. The Smarter Balanced tests are designed to test critical thinking and analysis through a mixture of multiple-choice, short answer, and extended response questions. California 3rd through 8th grade students and 11th grade students field tested the examination in 2014. The Field Test was a practice run that allowed teachers and students to gain experience with computerized assessments aligned to the Common Core before they were implemented in 2015.

2014—Election of Jerry Brown

Jerry Brown is serving his fourth term as governor of California. He was first elected in 1976 and served two terms. Twenty-seven years later in 2010, he was elected for his third term and re-elected in 2014 for his fourth term. Brown has been a leader in his support of education. He lists his major educational achievement as the approval of Proposition 30. This proposition provided major funding for California schools and colleges that was discussed earlier in this chapter.

2016—Proposition 55—Extension of Proposition 30

The additional tax on California taxpayers making more than $250,000 per year was scheduled to end in 2019. However, with the support of teachers, parents, and the educational community, Proposition 55 was placed on the ballot in 2016. It was approved by voters and extended the tax to 2030.

SUMMARY

California citizens expressed an early commitment to education. This commitment was formalized in California's first constitution with the requirement that each district provide a public school.

A major factor in the history of California's public education has been the state's attempts to cope with the problems associated with increased student enrollment. This challenge became particularly acute with the coming of World War II and continues into the 21st century.

The balance of this chapter offered a discussion of educational issues with a focus on school finance that came to the fore in the second half of the 20th century and continues to shape financing of public education in California. Perhaps the most significant change occurred in 1978 with the passage of Proposition 13, when a shift was made from local finance of education by property taxes to state financial support of education with a mix of state income tax, state sales tax, and property tax. This means of financing public education has continued into the 21st century. The chapter contained a discussion of other legislation, initiatives, and programs designed by state leaders that have shaped and molded California's public education.

KEY TERMS

After-School Education
   and Safety Program
Assembly Bill 65
Assembly Bill 484
California High School Exit
   Exam (CAHSEE)
Common Core Standards
Gann Limit
Morgan-Hart Class Size
   Reduction
Proposition 13
Proposition 20
Proposition 30
Proposition 38
Proposition 39

Proposition 49
Proposition 98
Proposition 111
Proposition 227
Senate Bill X51
Senate Bill 90
Senate Bill 376
Senate Bill 813
Senate Bill 1468
Senate Bill 1777
Serrano v. Priest
Smarter Balanced Assessment
STAR Program
Teacher Peer Assistence and
      Review Program (PAR)

Discussion/Essay Questions

1. The story of public education in California is largely dominated by the state attempting to cope with ever-increasing numbers of students. With hindsight, should the state have provided greater resources to local school districts to assist in the construction of schools? Justify your answer. If you believe greater resources should have been provided by the state, what would have been the source of the funds?

2. Discuss the pros and cons of the equal funding of California school districts that resulted from the *Serrano v. Priest* decision.

3. Give two arguments in favor of Proposition 13 and two opposing arguments.

4. Proposition 227 virtually ended the state's bilingual education program. Give two persuasive and two opposing arguments for the proposition.

California Education: Challenges and Opportunities

California is more than a geographical or political state. It is also a state of mind, a way of life and an evolving dream.

(Kevin Starr, Historian and Retired State Librarian of California, quoted in Los Angeles Times, *March 27, 2003)*

Introduction

Government institutions, including the United States government, state governments, and school districts, are similar to private organizations in that each institution faces an array of challenges. Some challenges are long-standing and ongoing, while new ones occur every day. Leaders of an institution exert a powerful influence on the ways in which challenges are met. The will and desire of the people exert a powerful influence on the shape and control of the institution itself. Many factors, including an institution's financial condition, its organizational structure, and its economic and social conditions, affect its reactions to the challenges that confront it.

In the case of California, state leadership has had a profound effect on education. The political ambitions of the governor and each legislator, his or her philosophy, judgement, and wisdom make an immense difference in the path the institution will take. The level of funding for schools, the curriculum and programs that are offered and required, and the nature of training and certification for teachers and other personnel are all influenced, if not determined, by state leadership.

A major factor in funding for a state's educational program is the wealth of that state. Are available tax dollars sufficient to build schools, employ teachers and staff, and provide essential instructional materials and facilities? Every state must grapple with providing resources for the many competing needs of its citizens: education, police and fire protection, health needs, adequate transportation, and so on.

Each state must make decisions about allocation of resources. In this process, education must compete with a multitude of demands. If a state does not have or is unwilling to allocate resources for education to cope with an increase in student enrollment, then per-pupil expenditures decline. A consequence of this financial decline may be difficulty in recruiting high caliber teachers and administrators. Other consequences may include increased class size, reduced funds for curriculum development, and inability to purchase essential books and instructional materials. Furthermore, school districts may have insufficient funds to maintain existing school facilities or to construct new school plants to accommodate increased student enrollment.

California schools face a unique set of challenges. California has more total students than other states, and a greater number of those are disadvantaged English Learners.

This chapter delineates some of the primary political, social, and economic challenges that influence the conditions of education in California. Among the many challenges with which California citizens must cope are the staggering numbers of students, and the diversity of the student body. Other issues include the recruitment of qualified teachers, and the financial ability and desire of California citizens to support education. These factors have had measurable effects upon the quality of education provided for California students. The following challenges are discussed in this chapter:

- Financial Crisis in public schools and recovery
- Control of California public schools
- Resources allocated to education
- Increasing population, especially the influx of minority students
- Academic achievement of California students
- The option and cost of class size reduction
- The direction and effect of virtual teaching and learning
- The growth and direction of the charter school movement
- Common Core Standards
- Successful implementation of new assessment program
- The challenge of financing special education
- The need to recruit, train, and evaluate California teachers

Financial Crisis in Public Schools and Recovery

The national recession that started in 2008 presented the most difficult challenge for states' financial management since the Great Depression. The recession resulted in a major drop in state revenue and loss of revenue for schools. As a result, schools across the country fired thousands of teachers, administrators, counselors, and support staff. Many states raised class size, reduced the number of school days, cut music and art programs, and eliminated after-school and summer school programs.

The National Association of State Budget Officers (NASBO, 2017) publishes an annual report, which contains information on the states' general fund receipts, expenditures, and balances. NASBO reports that the fiscal crisis was beginning to subside for most states by 2016–2017. However, the economic recovery is relatively weak compared to other post-recessionary periods.

California schools have shared to some extent in that recovery. When the recession started in 2008, the average school district received $8,595 per student. As recently as 2013–2014, that amount was $126 less than 2008 at $8,469. However, with the improved economy and the passage of Proposition 30 and 55, the amount was increased to $10,910 in the 2017-2018 budget (EdSource, 2017).

To some extent, California schools have shared in that recovery. When the recession started in 2008, the average school district received $8,595 per student. However, with the improved economy and the passage of Proposition 30 and 55, the amount increased to $10,910 in the 2017-2018 budget (California Budget, 2017).

Control of California Public Schools

As noted in Chapter 2, the control of schools has largely shifted from local school boards to the governor and state legislature. Political scientists and policymakers have long been concerned about the consolidation of political power in Sacramento. Those who believe in local control have expressed anxiety, and often frustration, as decision-making has shifted from local governments to the state.

A major shift in financial control of school districts occurred with passage of Senate Bill 90 in 1972. This legislation established a formula for maximum per-pupil income for school districts and took away the authority of local school boards to increase taxes. For this formula, the state established the term "revenue limit."

State control was further expanded with the passage of Proposition 13 in June of 1978. This proposition amended the state constitution to restrict annual ad valorem taxes to 1% of a property's market value and limited the conditions under which property assessments could be increased. Proposition 13 gave local school boards very few revenue enhancement powers. Local voters were denied the opportunity to levy ad valorem taxes in excess of the 1% rate except when bonds were approved. Until the year 2000, even this power was limited by the requirement of a 2/3 vote. However, at that time Proposition 39 lowered the requirement to 55%.

Financial Condition of the State and Its People

California has a diverse economy—the largest in the nation. Texas, at 60% the size of California's economy, ranks second. If California were a separate nation, it would rank sixth in the world, exceeded only by the United States, Japan, China, Germany, France, and Brazil (U.S. Census Bureau, 2017). The U.S. Department of Commerce (2016) estimates per capita income in California at $56,374—sixth in the nation. But do Californians pay a greater share of that wealth in taxes when compared to other states?

Anti-tax organizations and the media have given California the image of a high tax state. To some extent, this image is justified. California does have a high income tax rate, particularly at the top income levels, as compared with other states. In 2017-2018 California had the sixth highest personal income tax rate in the United States (Tax Foundation, 2017).

It should be noted that comparing states as to taxes paid by citizens is extremely complex because tax rates change frequently and deductions differ from state to state. Moreover, taxes may vary from county to county and city to city within a state. For example, the state sales tax may be 6%, but in some states, local counties or cities may have the power to add to that rate by as much as 4%. In addition, some figures include transfers from the federal government while others do not.

Table 2	Revenue Sources in California with California's Rank among the 50 States	
Tax	**California Rank[1]**	**Comment**
Property Tax	13	No change
Personal Income Tax	6	No change
Sales Tax	43	No change
Gasoline Tax	7	No change
Alcoholic Beverage Tax	28	No change
Wine Tax	43	No change

[1]States are ranked by revenues as a percent of personal income
Rankings from Tax Foundation (2017)

With the caveat that these numbers can and will change almost overnight, California's rankings on various taxes at the time of this writing are presented in Table 2.

Resources Allocated to Education

Schools are big business; in fact, they are the third largest business in California, trailing only aerospace and agriculture in total annual expenditures. In the 1960s, California public schools were the envy of the country and the world. In 1978, California's funding of education was 20% above the national average. That year the state ranked 17th nationwide in per-pupil expenditures. Education was among California's growth industries and one of its highest priorities. California universities were consistently ranked at the very top in the nation and the world. California public schools had little to fear from parent or community dissatisfaction with public education.

California's expenditures per pupil, in comparison to the rest of the nation, began to decline in the late 1970s and early 1980s. The state's ranking fell to an all-time low of 44th in 2008-2009. The state's position improved to 21st in 2016 at $11,330 per pupil, compared to the national average of $16,310. Vermont, which ranked number one in expenditures for education, was spending $19,337 for each student (NEA, 2017).

The problem is not lack of means. Even though California has higher taxes, it spends proportionately less on K-12 schools than many other states. A state's support of the various services can be measured by the amount it spends on services per $1,000 of personal income.

While California ranks lower in per-capita expenditures for education, it ranks much higher in several other categories. For example, California ranks fourth in spending for prisons and sixth in police and fire protection. It ranks eleventh in expenditures for healthcare (NEA, 2017).

The monies available per pupil affect the number of students per classroom, the amount spent on teachers' salaries, and other items that directly alter the learning experiences of students. Another major result of limited school funding is that school districts and communities must deal with uncertainty, knowing that reductions are often necessary to balance the district budget.

Increase in State Population

A brief summary of California's population growth will assist the reader in understanding the state's ongoing challenge in providing for its citizens. In 1850 when statehood was achieved, the population was less than 100,000. By 1900 this figure had jumped to 1,485,053 and by 1940 to 6,907,387. In 1960, only twenty years later, the population had more than doubled to 15,717,204. It almost doubled again to 29,760,021 in 1990.

By the time of the 2000 census, California's population numbered 33,871,648 and increased to 39,524,000 by January 1, 2017. The department projects that California's population will reach 44 million in 2030 and 51 million by 2060. The yearly increase of population is roughly equal to the total combined population of San Bernardino and Sacramento counties—or the entire state of Wyoming (CDF, 2017).

California's Hispanic population became the dominant ethnic group in 2014. The Department of finance projects that the Hispanic population will increase to 41 percent of the state's population by 2020, while the white population will make-up less than 37 percent (CDF, 2017).

Student Population

The California Department of Finance (CDF, 2017) predicts that over the next ten years, California's public K-12 school enrollment will grow by less than one percent to reach a total of 6,264,000 students. This increase will add 45,800 students by 2022-2023. The increase in enrollment will occur mostly at the secondary level. Elementary enrollment will remain fairly steady with a slight increase by 2022-2023.

In 2016-2017 there were 1,024 California school districts and 10,477 schools (CDE, 2017). The schools were managed by 23,140 administrators, 26,367 support staff, and 274,246 teachers. In addition, there were 1,019 Charter Schools with an enrollment of 438,474 students (CDE, 2017).

Increase in Minority Students

A major challenge and opportunity for California educators is the ethnic and linguistic diversity of students enrolled in the public schools. The California Department of Education projects that school enrollment will continue to diversify. For example, between 2000-2001 and 2016-2017, the number of white students declined by 14% and that of African-American by 2%, whereas the Hispanic student population increased by 14% (CDE, 2017).

Along with ethnic diversity, there is a wide variety of languages spoken in the state. In 2016-2017 (CDE, 2017) English learners were a significant portion of public school enrollment. There were more than a million English learners, which represented 22% of the total enrollment in California public schools.

Almost three million students speak a language other than English in their homes. That number is about 43% of the state's enrollment. The majority are enrolled in the elementary grades, kindergarten through grade 6. The additional 28% are secondary students. The majority of English learners, 85%, speak Spanish (CDE, 2017). With the increase in the number of students whose primary language is not English, a major challenge is finding the best way to teach these young people and providing primary language support, developing English fluency, and preparing students for the daily demands of an unfamiliar environment.

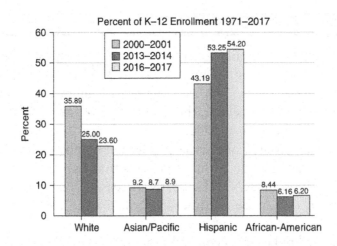

Figure 1   Change in Ethnic Distribution
SOURCE: California Departments of Education and Finance, 2016–2017.

Student Achievement

Most educators agree that improving student achievement is the number one priority, and this task has been a major challenge in California. To measure student achievement, students took a battery of tests. From 1998 to 2012, California students took a series of tests, called the STAR Program (Standardized Testing and Reporting). As discussed earlier in the text, this program was ended in 2013. The state testing was ended to prepare students for the new Smarter Balanced assessments, which is aligned to the Common Core Standards.

In addition to the state testing program, the National Assessment of Education Progress (NAEP) completes national and state tests at least once every two years in reading and math in grades four through eight. This program is commonly referred to as "The Nation's Report Card." For more than 30 years information on what students know and can do has been generated by the NAEP. This test provides states with test scores and a comparison of the state's results with other states.

California students do not perform well on the national test, and student achievement in basic skills ranks below the national average. In reading, California's fourth grade reading scores were lower than 49 other states. Eighth grade students did not do much better, having scores lower than 47 other states. California students did about the same in math as they did with reading. Fourth graders ranked 49, and eighth grade students ranked 44 (NAEP, 2015).

California leaders, citizens, parents, and students face a major challenge to improve student achievement. It will take a major effort of the state and its people to ensure that students are prepared for full citizenship and the world of work.

Class Size

After several decades, the teacher-student ratio in California increased until it was the second highest in the nation. In 1996-1997 Governor Pete Wilson and the legislature took action, allocating funds to hold classes at 20 students in kindergarten through grade three. However, over the years, class size increased and was the highest in the nation in 2012-2013 (NEA, 2013).

California teachers work with more students each day than teachers in most other states—23 per classroom as compared to the national average of 16 (NEA, 2016). The situation is even more grim with the number of students per counselor and librarian, with California last in the those two categories. The California budget Project (2013) reports that California ranks 48th with the number of students per administrator.

A major challenge for educators is to verify objectively that class size reduction actually results in improving student achievement. If class size reduction does improve student achievement, the next goal for the citizens of the state must be to provide the resources to carry class size reduction through all grades.

Common Core Standards

Teachers and educational leaders have argued for decades that the nation's students need to improve academic achievement in order to compete with the rest of the world. As early as the 1950s, President Eisenhower called for national standards, and other presidents including George H.W. Bush, Bill Clinton, and George Bush supported the concept. However, none of the presidents were able to persuade Congress or the nation to adopt national standards (Pullmann, 2013).

Rather than national standards, each state adopted state standards for grade levels and subjects. California adopted state standards in 1998. Those who favored national standards continued their work and achieved partial success in 2008. In that year, a consortium of states developed and shared standards. This task was led by the National Governors Association and the Council of Chief State School Officers, which adopted the new standards. By 2014, 45 states had adopted the K–12 standards, referred to as Common Core. Education Next (West, 2018) reports that support for using the same academic standards across the states has increased, as long as the "brand name" of Common Core is not mentioned.

The goal of the advocacy groups was to establish national standards of what children should know in each grade and subject from kindergarten to high school graduation. They argued that students would benefit from national standards, rather than each state establishing its own standards. They argued that common standards would help make U.S. students more competitive with students in other nations.

A majority of the nation's superintendents are optimistic about the Common Core Standards. Almost 100% see the new standards as more rigorous than previous standards. The superintendents expressed concern that states and school districts will have adequate resources to implement the standards to ensure student learning (EdCal, 2014).

The California School Board approved the Common Core Standards in 2010 with implementation in 2014–2015.The goal of Common Core is to offer more relevant, practical, and rigorous lessons and to teach students to solve problems and think critically. Governor Brown demonstrated his support for Common Core by including $1.25 billion in one-time funding in the 2013–2014 state budget. The funds were used by school districts for professional development, technology, and instructional materials.

The major questions regarding the Common Core Standards are: Will the standards result in the desired result of improving student achievement? Will citizens and education leaders be able to implement the standards, with growing opposition from those who claim that the standards will result in a national curriculum?

California Assessment of Student Performance and Progress (CAASPP)

California's Standardized Testing and reporting (STAR) Program was replaced with the CASSPP and a new test, "Smarter Balanced." In 2014-2015, California and 24 other states used the test. By 2016-2017 this number had dropped to 15 states that used this test (Gevertz, 2017).

The new test is aligned with the Common Core Standards. The tests used in the STAR program were multiple choice, except for writing assessments in grades 4 and 7. The Smarter Balanced tests are designed to test critical thinking and analysis through a mix of multiple-choice, short answer, and extended response questions. California 3rd through 8th grade students and 11th grade students field tested the examination in 2014. The field test was a practice run that allowed teachers and students to gain experience with the computerized test aligned to the Common Core Standards before implementation in 2015.

An example of a question from the new test: A 10th grade student is asked to develop a report on the pros and cons of limiting the use of fossil fuel, and the effects of that decision, the student is asked to research the issue and write an essay arguing for limiting the use of fossil fuel and to provide support for the decision.

In 2017 the State Superintendent of Public Instruction (CDE, 2017) announced that scores in English language arts and mathematics remained steady and retained the strong gains made in 2016. Almost 50 percent of students met or exceeded the English language arts/literacy standards, and almost 40 percent did as well on the math test.

Virtual Teaching/Learning

Perhaps the most revolutionary change in education since the invention of printing is the Internet. Will the Internet replace school campuses, textbooks, and teachers within the next few years? Sounds far-fetched–but perhaps not.

Historically, American student learning opportunities have been limited by geography and the ability of parents to purchase a home in a school district noted for excellence. Online learning has basically eliminated these two restrictions. Twenty-first century students are children of the digital age, and many are more comfortable with technology than their parents and teachers.

Online learning is increasing rapidly across the United States as more and more students and educators become familiar with the benefits of learning unconstrained by geography and time. Forty-eight states and the District of Columbia offer online courses to some students. In most cases, online courses are blended with in-school courses.

An example of the benefit of online learning is demonstrated by Bob Wise, former governor of West Virginia. Mr. Wise attended a graduation ceremony at Pickens High School in Randolph County, a school where the graduating class consisted of two students. Mr. Wise asked the principal how he was able to hire foreign language teachers. The principal said the school has one of the best Spanish teachers in the country. She teaches her class everyday from San Antonio, Texas (Harrison, D., 2011).

An example of a California virtual learning program is the University of California, University California College Prep (UCCP) program. This program was started in 1999 and was created to develop and provide quality courses offered free to participating school districts. UCCP has provided the courses as a supplement to teachers and over 150,000 California students have made us of this resource. UCCP offers access to over 40 courses, including "a-g" and general high school courses (UCCP, 2010).

California has a wide range of online college options in multiple subjects at all educational levels. In 2016, all 33 colleges and universities that make up the University of California (UC) and California State University (CSU) systems offered the distance learning option.

California community colleges offer more online instruction than any other public higher-education institution in the United States. In 2012 online course enrollment in California's community colleges totaled almost one million, about 11% of total enrollment. A 2014 study by the Public Policy Institute of California (Johnson & Mejia, 2014) found mixed achievement by online students. Students are less likely to complete and pass an online course than a traditional course.

However, students who take at least some online courses are more likely than those who take only traditional courses to earn an associate's degree or transfer to a four-year college. Governor Brown has proposed spending tens of millions of dollars to promote online learning, while others will question this expenditure.

The research and arguments, both pro and con, as the educational value of learning online will continue unabated for some time, but visions of no school construction, no school buses, no textbooks, no school lunches, and no school principal are powerful financial stimuli to make such programs work.

Charter Schools

A public charter school is a publicly funded school that is typically governed by a group or organization under a legislative contract or charter with the state. The charter exempts the school from selected state or local rules and regulations. In return for funding and autonomy, the charter school must meet the accountability standards contained in the charter. A school's charter is reviewed periodically every three to five years and can be revoked if guidelines are not followed or if the standards are not met. In 2016-2017, Charter Schools operated in 43 states and the District of Columbia (NAPCS, 2017).

From 2003-2004 to 2016-2017, the number of students enrolled in public charter schools tripled from 789,000 to over 2.6 million (NAPCS, 2017). The percentage of public schools that were charter schools increased from 2% to 5%.

The intent of the charter movement is to facilitate parent choice and more rapid innovation within the public school system. The expectation is that if educators are freed from regulation by the district and the state, quality will improve. The legislation is revolutionary in terms of the freedom from state laws and regulations that has been granted to charter schools.

California was the second state to authorize charter schools: Minnesota was first in 1991. In 1992, Senator Gary Hart introduced legislation that permitted up to 100 schools to be identified as charter schools. The California charter schools are governed by their charter petitions but are otherwise exempt from all state laws regulating education, except those that relate to the State Teachers' Retirement System and new laws that are approved, particularly regarding the governance of the schools.

A 1998 amendment permitted 250 additional charters in that year and 100 additional charters in each subsequent year. Thus in 1993-1994 there were 85 charter schools. By 2016-2017 that number had grown to 1,253. California's charter school enrollment in that year was 604,700. The state of Texas had the second largest enrollment with 345,200 students at charter schools (NAPCS, 2017).

Any individual may petition a school board for permission to form a school as long as 10% of the teachers in a district, or 50% of the teachers in a school agree. Since 1998, it has also been possible to apply for a charter if half the parents or teachers in the proposed school sign a petition. An appeal process is included in the event a school board declines to approve a charter.

State funding may be funneled through the district or transferred directly to the charter school in an amount matching the base revenue limit of the district. In addition to the base revenue, the school may also apply for categorical aid. Charter schools are required to submit fiscal reports to their "chartering authority" (district or state) and allow the county superintendent of schools to monitor their financial management.

Although Americans are expressing strong support for charter schools, do students in charter schools outperform their peers in traditional schools? The Huffington Post (2014) reports that the research is mixed. Research indicates that charter schools do not outperform their traditional public schools.

While the research on student achievement in charter schools is mixed, the message is clear that the continued increase in charter school enrollment shows satisfaction with the program by students and parents.

Special Education

In 1975, the U.S. Congress approved Education for All Handicapped Children (now know as Individuals with Disabilities Education Act (IDEA). This legislation provided that all children with disabilities receive a free, appropriate public education. Congress knew that it was creating a law that would have a financial impact at the state and local level. Congress agreed to pay for the excess costs of educating a child with a disability.

It has been more than four decades since the passage of this legislation, the federal contribution has fallen far short of the congressional commitment to support special education services. The IDEA typically covers less than 20% of the 40% originally committed by the federal government. The California's Legislative Analyst estimates that California would receive $2 billion more annually if the federal government to funded special education at the level originally committed by the federal government (LAO, 2013).

The National Center for Education Statistics, (NCES, 2013) reports that in 2010–2012, 6.5 million (16%) of the nation's students received special-needs services. In that same year, California served almost seven million (10%) special needs students (LAO, 2013).

Keenan and Associates, the largest privately held insurance brokerage and consulting firm in California, stated that spiraling costs for special education are dealing a devastating blow to California public schools. In many districts, special education costs exceed the revenue provided to the district from state, federal, and local sources (Keenan, 2010).

An example is the Hemet Unified School District, located in Southern California. In order to receive federal funds, the district must meet maintenance of effort requirements. This standard required the district's contributions to its special education program to be at least the same level as the previous year. Therefore, Hemet's 2013–2014 budget allocation to special education from the general funds was in excess of eight million dollars (Hemet, 2013).

Most Americans support providing special services to students with disabilities. The debate becomes "who pays?" The federal government mandates the service, but has not provided adequate funds to support the program. Many parents believe the federal and state governments provide special education funding and some even assume that special education is entirely funded by the federal government. The bottom line is that the local school district is primarily responsible for special education. The challenge is how to fund the program.

Facilities

There is not a national database for information on public school facilities. Some states collect information, and some do not. A national organization, American Society of Civil Engineers, (ASCE, 2017) reports that nearly 50 million K-12 students and six million adults occupy 100,000 school buildings. This organization estimates that 24 percent of public school buildings are in fair or poor condition. The ASCE cites several examples such as leaking roofs, poor ventilation and lighting, and plumbing that are a constant problem.

President Trump made rebuilding the nation's infrastructure an important part of his presidential campaign and has included this goal in several speeches since his election. A major goal of the president's plan is to grow the economy and to create jobs. The Secretary of Transportation stated that rebuilding roads, bridges and schools is a priority, but has offered few details regarding the Trump plan (Jenkins, 2017).

While the nation's infrastructure earned a "D+" in the ASCE Infrastructure Report Card, California faces infrastructure challenges of its own. The need for school facilities in California, and plans to meet the needs, are discussed in Chapter 15 of this text.

Teacher Shortage and Recruitment

Over the past several decades the nation has experienced a shortage of teachers from time to time. When the economy turns down, teachers are laid-off, and when the economy recovers there is a shortage of teachers. The National Department of Education (NEA, 2017) reports that the current shortage of teachers started with the recession of 2008-2009 when thousands of teachers received lay-off notices. With the layoffs, students who were planning a teaching career became discouraged and often choose another career path.

In 2016-2017 almost every state reported a shortage of teachers. This shortage is particularly acute in math, special education, science, and foreign language (U.S. Department of Education, 2017).

California joins other states in not being able to fill the classrooms with qualified teachers in the above categories. In 2016-2017 the state added the position of elementary teacher to the list of shortages. The California Department of Education (CDE, 2017) projected a need to hire 23,000 new teachers in 2016-2017. However, the California Teaching Commission issued fewer than 16,000 new credentials that year leaving a shortage of 7,000 vacancies. Of the credentials issued, almost 4,000 came from out of state. To combat the shortage, the Commission also issued intern credentials and provisional permits (EdCal, 2017).

In comparison, there were 21,750 credentials issued in 2008-2009 and 15,547 issued in 2015-2016. An even more disturbing trend is that the number of students enrolled in teacher preparation programs has decreased by more than 20 percent in the past five years (CTC, 2017).

It is obvious that a solution must be found to provide each California classroom with a qualified teacher during the next decade. In addition to the problems cited, the replacement of teachers who plan to retire will be a significant challenge. In 2015-2016, the California Department of Education reported that almost 20 percent of California teachers were over age 55 (CDE, 2017). Most of these can be expected to retire within the next decade.

Research clearly demonstrates that teacher quality is one of the most important factors in student achievement. California governors, with concurrence of the state legislature, provided several incentives to recruit and train California teachers. Some of these measures included the establishment of teacher recruitment centers, teacher internships, and loans for down payments on homes.

Other incentives include extra compensation for teachers who are willing to work in low performing schools, tax incentives for teachers, forgiveness of loans, and funds to train teachers to obtain certification for subject areas where shortages exist. Sadly, with all the other demands for tax dollars, these programs are in jeopardy.

SUMMARY

The residents of California face formidable educational challenges during this decade. Most educators and citizens are in agreement that the greatest challenge is to improve student achievement—achievement that will prepare students for responsible citizenship, success in college and the world of work, and a productive life. While there is little argument about the importance of improved student achievement, opinion is not unanimous regarding how to achieve the goal or how to finance it.

Among the challenges are limits on the amount of tax dollars allocated to education; increased enrollment; the particular needs of minority students, especially English learners; and the needs of children born into poverty. Other issues include demands for new and remodeled facilities, the direction and effect of virtual teaching and learning, and the training and recruitment of teachers.

KEY TERMS

Budget for education

CAASPP

Charter schools

Class size

Common Core

Control of public schools

Facilities

Minority students

Per capita personal income

Per-pupil expenditures

Resources allocated for public schools

State population

Special education students

Student achievement

Teacher shortage

Virtual teaching/learning

Discussion/Essay Questions

1. In 1978, California ranked 17th nationwide in per-pupil expenditures for education. By 2008–2009, the state was in 44th place. Discuss three major reasons for this decline in California's ranking.

2. While California ranks near the bottom of the states in total tax receipts spent on education, it ranks much higher in per capita expenditures for public health, police protection, and public welfare. Discuss three major reasons for this disparity.

3. California has an increasing percentage of students representing ethnic minorities. What implications does this fact have for California school finance?

4. Although California workers achieve a median income 12% higher than the national average, poverty among California children falls 15% above the national average. Is this appropriate? Discuss arguments pro and con. Consider ways this apparent imbalance might be changed.

Role of the Chief Business Officer

Introduction

California schools are big business. In 2017-2018 the general fund was $74 billion. Almost 40 percent of that amount is allocated for K-12 education. These funds are distributed to more than 1,000 districts, charter schools, and 58 counties. In many communities, the school district is the primary industry with the largest number of employees and the highest payroll.

California has three types of public school districts: elementary, secondary, and unified. Elementary districts may contain grades K–6 or K–8; secondary districts include grades 7–12 or 9–12; and unified districts contain all grades from K through 12. The number of districts changes as districts unify or as a district divides to form two or more separate districts. For example, dividing the Los Angeles Unified School District into several smaller districts has been discussed for many years.

In 2016-2017 there were 528 Elementary Districts, 76 High School Districts and 344 Unified Districts. In addition, there were 58 County Office Schools, and a small number of specialized schools like California Youth Authority, state Special Schools, and state charter schools (CDE, 2017).

This chapter discusses the person responsible for the day-to-day management of this significant commitment of California taxpayers. As the previous sections of this text indicate, the pressure on school boards, superintendents, and staff has increased significantly as a result of the "squeeze" on financial resources for California schools. The complexities of school accounting, major legislation, and ballot initiatives also account for major stress on districts and their leadership. All but the smallest districts employ a chief business official (CBO) to manage the district's financial resources. In districts with very few employees, financial management may be the responsibility of the superintendent. The superintendent, in this case, is usually assisted in financial matters by a private consultant or a consultant from the county schools office. As enrollment increases warrant additional staff, first priority is usually placed on employing a business official. This need typically takes precedence over hiring a staff member to manage personnel or instruction.

Title and Preparation

Few professions have risen so far and so fast as that of school business manger. As recently as 20 years ago, the post was virtually unknown. Today, even the smallest districts have someone in that role who is an important part of the leadership team. The position is likely to increase as districts become more and more autonomous.

There is little consistency in titles of chief business officials in California school districts. The CBO may be designated the assistant superintendent of business, business manager, director of business, associate superintendent of business, or director of fiscal services. This variety of titles is due, in part, to a lack of certification requirements for the CBO. While the personnel officer and head of instruction must hold California teaching and administrative credentials, no credential is necessary for the head of the business department.

Business officials also bring to their assignments a wide variety of experience and training. Although a number of school business officials have teaching and administrative backgrounds, many lack such formal experience and training. A substantial number of business leaders possess training in business and accounting; a majority hold a college or university degree. However, a significant number do *not* have a college or university degree and gain their positions through experience. Many CBOs have been promoted after gaining experience in the business department as a payroll or purchasing clerk or in an accounting position.

There is a major difference between the work of a school business manager and a business official in private enterprise. In the private sector the business manager is concerned with a profit margin and is judged by how effectively that objective is achieved. The school business manager's objective is less well-defined. The product of a school system, its students, is not as easily measured or evaluated as the profit in a business ledger. Perhaps that explains, in part, why school business officials find that they do not receive the same respect or financial remuneration as their counterparts in the private sector.

Many California public and private universities provide training for aspiring school business managers or chief business officials. It is common for a university to offer a certificate in school business management. Ordinarily, these programs do not require candidates to possess a college degree, but rather some experience in accounting, finance or management. This program attracts many employees who work in a school district, like accounting, payroll, transportation, and food service.

The certificate programs generally include the skills identified by the California Association of School Business Officials (CASBO) or the requirements of the National Association of School Business Officers (ASBO). An example of classes that are taught in the school business management program at California State University, San Bernardino include finance and budgeting, accounting, facilities planning, and managing the classified employees program. The classes are on the weekends or evenings and taught by full-time professors and practicing school administrators.

The salary for Chief Business Officials has significantly increased in recent years and now exceeds $100,000 in many districts. For example, five openings were listed for business manager or chief financial officer in the July, 2014 CASBO Finder; the salaries ranged from \$142,867 to \$190,162. The highest salary was a large district, Long Beach California Unified.

In 2001 the Association of School Business Officials International adopted a set of professional standards covering seven areas:

- the educational enterprise
- financial resource management
- human resource management
- facility management
- property acquisition and management
- information management
- ancillary services, including risk management, transportation, and food service (Abner, 2003).

Of these, financial resource management was deemed most important by chief state school officers. These officials believed that a school business certificate program (52% of respondents) or better yet, a master's degree in school business management (64%), would be beneficial to practitioners in their states (Wanger, 2003).

Duties and Responsibilities

The role of the school business manager has changed significantly over the years, from that of bookkeeper to the increasingly complex and technical responsibility of accounting for the many programs offered by a school district. Job descriptions place the district's financial officer in a support role, rather than a line position, with respect to certificated staff. The business department exists to provide assistance to administrators and teachers with direct responsibility for education of students.

Both a review of the literature and an examination of sample CBO job descriptions reveal similarities in duties and responsibilities required of the CBO in various settings. The first responsibility of the position is providing resources for an efficient and effective educational program, a staff role.

However, the CBO has direct line—or supervisory—responsibility for the business office, maintenance and operations, transportation, and food services. Tasks under the direction of the CBO typically include strategic planning; financial planning and budgeting; information technology; collective bargaining; fiscal accounting, reports, and auditing; payroll; purchasing and warehousing; insurance and risk management; facilities management; and providing fiscal information to the board of education, superintendent, and site administrators. Each of these areas of responsibility is discussed on the following pages.

Strategic Planning

With school finance changing each year, many administrators feel that long-range financial plans are almost impossible. Nevertheless, successful districts develop long-range plans, sometimes referred to as strategic plans. What are the financial objectives for the district and what are the strategies for achieving these objectives? Obviously, with a school district dependent on so many outside sources for revenue, strategic planning is not an easy task.

The effective strategic plan must include several assumptions and "what if" scenarios. For example, lottery income per pupil was its highest ever in 1988–89, when it hit $176 per pupil. Two years later, the state Lottery Commission projected an income of approximately $160 per pupil for 1990–91, then subsequently revised that estimate to $127. The following year, lottery income fell to its lowest level thus far: $77 per pupil.

A CBO that constructed the budget on the $127 dollars would have had to scramble to make up the difference. While the lottery accounts for less than 2% of a district's income, it is clearly an undependable figure (CDE, 2007). See additional discussion of the California lottery in Chapter 6, School District Revenue.

A more recent example of the need for strategic planning occurred in August 2007 when the Board voted to extend the schedule of part-time cafeteria workers to four hours a day. That change immediately qualified 2,352 workers for health benefits at a cost of 35 million dollars per year.

The Los Angeles superintendent was asked repeatedly where he would find the 35 million dollars. The superintendent did not respond, but noted that the cafeteria fund was already in the red. Supporters of the health insurance for the cafeteria workers noted that the funds could be made up by encouraging more students to eat school food. Currently, only 35% of secondary school students eat in the cafeteria (Blume, August 31, 2007).

To cite another example, electricity costs in California tripled during the 2000–01 school year. CBOs began a frantic search for funds to pay the utilities, since that account had been under-budgeted in the budget just adopted. A good strategic plan would have included the possibility of reduced lottery funds and increased utility bills and would have maintained a reserve for such contingencies.

Many sources of information contribute to a strategic plan. In addition to the usual enrollment projections and data from the county and state, the business manager should subscribe to one of several legislative updates. The CBO should also observe the economy closely by reading daily newspapers such as the *Wall Street Journal*, the *Los Angeles Times*, and the *San Francisco Chronicle*. Several CBOs subscribe to *Barron's* and *Forbes* magazines for the same reason. In addition to business reports, a number of professional journals in education should be "must" reading; valuable resources include the CASBO *Journal of School Business Management*, *School Business Affairs* from American School Business Officials International, *Phi Delta Kappan*, and *Educational Leadership*.

To affect an organization, a strategic plan must be widely disseminated to the staff and community. If the plan includes something like refurbishing a gymnasium every five years at a cost in excess of half a million dollars, the community can be encouraged to develop a mind-set that recognizes this need. All successful plans should include a source of funds for each project. If refurbishing the gym includes a community election to pass an assessment tax, one must plan early to gain support for the project.

The most important objective of planning is to enable decision-makers to focus on the big picture, or long-range needs, and not just to react from one crisis to the next. Developing and effectively communicating a long-range plan for a district is probably one of the greatest challenges to the business manager.

Financial Planning and Budgeting

The district's CBO has a major responsibility for examining the district's goals, ensuring that they are student-centered, and calculating the dollars needed to accomplish those goals (White, 1997). The annual budget is one of the most important documents in any district. It is a blueprint of the district's priorities for that year. The budget should be based on sound objectives and contain well-supported assumptions for projected income and expenditures. As a financial plan that details a district's objectives, the budget should be developed and written to communicate those objectives to staff and citizens of the community.

Financial planning properly considers district needs several years into the future. These needs include the instructional program, facilities, maintenance and operations, and all other aspects of an effective program for students. The plans should be translated into revenue projections and expenditures, yet remain flexible as district needs change.

Information Technology

A major change in the role of the CBO occurred with the advent of information technology. The computer age started after World War II, but did not impact school financial operations until the mid-50s. The first use was to prepare payroll and accounting records. By 1965 mainframe computers were utilized by county offices and larger school districts. By 1975 personal computers started appearing in districts, and by 1985 most middle-size to larger districts were using personal computers in district offices, at school sites, and in some classrooms. By 1995 the majority of districts had developed some network-based systems, and at the turn of the century most districts had installed connections to the Internet (Malone, 1998).

Today a major portion of a CBO's daily work is done on a computer. Prior to the computer age, a district's financial reports were often complex and too detailed for management and board use. The computer has made it possible to prepare simplified financial information by utilizing graphs, charts, and spreadsheets. The amount of data generated in the future will make it even more important for the CBO to be effective in analyzing, preparing, and presenting data.

Collective Bargaining

Collective bargaining has become a major responsibility of CBOs in the past 25 years. The vast majority of California school district employees are members of a labor union. These unions have been most effective in lobbying for school resources. For example, the California Teachers Association was primarily responsible for the passage of Proposition 98, which provided school districts a minimum fixed amount of the state budget each year. Employee organizations carry clout with state legislators and the governor. Members of teacher and classified organizations often play a significant role in the election of local school board members.

Obviously, work with employee associations significantly influences the work of the CBO. Labor relations is a very time-consuming task, and the CBO's preparation of accurate information and the presentation of that information in credible fashion is critical in the collective bargaining process.

Fiscal Accounting, Reports, and Auditing

This set of tasks has become increasingly complex. Many CBOs would argue that the task is extremely burdensome, involving many reports required by county, state, and federal agencies. Although most districts have business staff to handle day-to-day accounting procedures, the CBO has final responsibility to ensure that all accounts and funds are properly documented and balanced. The successful CBO regularly presents to the superintendent and school board a status report on the district's financial condition.

As discussed in a later section of this text, California requires school districts to have all accounts and funds audited on a yearly basis by an independent auditor. The county superintendent of schools is also charged with monitoring school district finances.

Payroll

In most California school districts, funds for salaries and benefits constitute a major portion of the budget. Indeed, in many districts approximately 80% of the budget is allocated to this area. Therefore, the CBO has a major obligation to establish effective payroll procedures to account for every expenditure in this budget category. Careful attention should be devoted to monitoring overtime, substitute hours, and temporary hires, as expenditures in these categories may gradually accumulate to significant amounts.

The CBO should be directly involved in the collective bargaining process and project the ongoing cost of salary increases and related expenditures. Fringe benefits, a budget item whose cost has accelerated significantly in the past several years, exemplify a major concern relative to a payroll.

Purchasing and Warehousing

The two major objectives of purchasing operations are to acquire supplies and equipment of the right quantity and quality and to obtain them at the lowest possible cost. To protect tax dollars, the legislature has enacted numerous rules and procedures to govern purchasing. As educational dollars decrease, the purchasing staff needs to go beyond legal requirements to provide instructional supplies for classrooms in adequate quantities and in timely fashion.

Careful analysis should be made of the advantages and disadvantages of establishing a district warehouse. Small districts may not find a warehouse cost-effective. As a rule of thumb, a warehouse becomes cost-effective when district enrollment approaches 5,000 students. However, this number is only a guideline, since particular circumstances, such as proximity to a major supplier or distances between schools, may influence the decision. Efficiency and cost control are the two key concepts in warehousing supplies and materials. Data processing equipment has enabled many districts to improve control over this business operation. Many districts are also using the Internet as a tool in the purchasing process.

Insurance and Risk Management

As with many other aspects of business management, providing adequate and affordable insurance has become so complex as to require special training. Millions of taxpayer dollars are spent each year on insurance of various kinds. It is important that carefully conceived management practices be established in this area. Many California districts have united in joint powers agreements or other cooperative arrangements to provide adequate insurance coverage.

Risk management is concerned with providing a safe environment to protect students and staff from injury. Over the last several years many districts have designated their CBO as the safety officer. In this role, the CBO establishes training programs on safety for students and staff. Theoretically, proper education, management, and control would eliminate all risks and hazards, but it is questionable whether any district can ever reach that condition. Nevertheless, a well-planned and managed safety program reduces injuries and losses.

Facilities Management

There are three issues in facilities management: new construction, maintaining facilities, and use of facilities. Each of these involves numerous laws, regulations, and procedures. A section later in this text is devoted to maintenance of facilities and construction of new facilities.

Criteria for use of facilities should be carefully outlined in district board policies and administrative procedures. Citizens of a community have paid for school facilities with tax dollars and are entitled to use them appropriately. By making adequate provision for access to school grounds, playfields, and classrooms, a district engenders strong community support for funds to maintain sites and to construct new schools.

Maintenance and Operations

A later section is devoted to this subject, but it is mentioned here as a responsibility assigned to most CBOs. The concept of "management by walking around" (MBWA) has become very popular in the last few years and perhaps should be a requirement in the job description of the CBO. Management by "walking on water" has also been suggested, but is difficult to implement! Regular visitations to school sites assist a CBO in identifying problems and create a basis for praising jobs well done—a most persuasive morale booster.

Transportation

A section on transportation also appears later in the text. The CBO, even in the smallest California school district, needs expert assistance in managing this department. Such assistance may come from a lead bus driver or shop assistant in a small district, from a transportation director in a large district. This department often employs a large staff and represents a substantial capital investment.

The successful CBO periodically seeks services from outside the district to review the performance of the transportation department. Such an independent audit helps ensure safe and efficient transportation of students and a cost-effective operation.

Food Service

Like transportation, food service is a support for students that usually falls under the aegis of the district's CBO. It, too, is a department highly regulated by state and federal legislation and other outside agencies. For example, county offices of education are responsible for ensuring that proper health standards are maintained in a district's kitchens and food service areas.

Many California districts contract with private business or with larger districts to provide this service. Each district has the primary duty of providing a nutritious meal for students at the lowest possible cost. Consultants from the county superintendent's office and the California Department of Education should be asked to complete a periodic review of the department to ensure that these objectives are being accomplished.

Board of Education, Superintendent, and Principals

The CBO, by training and experience, is uniquely qualified to keep the board, superintendent, and principals informed of the financial condition of the district. It is the CBO's task to warn of the financial consequences of a "great instructional idea" that the district may be unable to afford.

It also falls on the shoulders of the CBO to play the "black hat" role in salary negotiations. The CBO is charged to analyze the effect of a cost-of-living increase on the current and long-term condition of the budget. He or she should clearly and, if necessary, forcefully inform all members of the board's negotiating team, the superintendent, and the board of education as to financial consequences of a proposed agreement. Better yet to work closely with all groups to keep them apprised of the financial situation of the district as it changes. In this way, a more collaborative style of management may be utilized.

A successful CBO should be a leading member of a superintendent's cabinet. The CBO keeps the superintendent and school board informed of all business matters. This is a major responsibility that requires expert knowledge of finance, legal requirements, and the myriad rules and regulations imposed on California school districts. The CBO must constantly remain aware of the changing financial scene, particularly of all relevant legislation under consideration in Sacramento.

Getting Started

What does one do in the first few days as a school business official? Quoting Dale Carnegie, Weeks (1999) counsels that listening and a commitment to helping others are critical to success. For the first ten days on the job, he recommends, in roughly this order:

- meeting colleagues to identify their perceptions and priorities
- noting the views of one's predecessor
- reviewing the district's financial picture
- locating records and noting where they are stored
- beginning to establish routines
- connecting to the local affiliate of the Association of School Business Officials International and to peers in other districts
- meeting the labor leaders in the district
- looking over the information management system
- getting a sense of the transportation system, being alert to problems
- finding out about the district's emergency response plans and procedures
- reading up-to-date reference materials
- developing a work plan and reviewing it with the superintendent.

Well, that should be enough to keep anyone busy!

SUMMARY

California chief business officials are "key players" in the successful management of a school district. The responsibility of the CBO is exceeded only by that of the superintendent. In many districts, the superintendent is dependent on the CBO in most financial matters.

The areas of responsibility of the CBO are numerous and complex. They range from maintaining the solvency of the district to managing the food services program. Expert planning and organizational abilities are "musts" for this important position. Every district has a major responsibility to employ a highly capable CBO who has the ability and skill to manage the district's resources competently and effectively.

KEY TERMS

Assistant Superintendent of Business

Budgeting

Business Manager

CBO

Director of Business

District warehouse

Financial planning

MBWA

Payroll

Purchasing

Risk management

Safety Officer

Strategic planning

Discussion/Essay Questions

1. Typically, in a small district the first assistant to the superintendent to be employed is a business manager. Discuss the major reasons for this decision.

2. California does not require a teaching or administrative credential for service as a business manager. Is this a good or poor decision? Explain your answer.

3. Responsibilities of the business manager have increased significantly in the past decade. Discuss three new tasks that have contributed to this increase in responsibilities.

4. Strategic planning is a major responsibility of the business manager. Discuss three major financial components that should be included in a district's strategic financial plan.

Managing the Budget

The single most important document of a California school district or county superintendent of schools is its annual budget—in effect, a road map to show how a school agency will fulfill its purpose and accomplish its aims.

(Charles Weis, Ventura County Superintendent of Schools)

Introduction

The state of California and all school districts are required to adopt a balanced budget each year. This chapter deals with the budgeting process. It concerns the role of the chief business officer in the process as well as legal budget guidelines, the work of the school financial resources committee, the requirement for interim reports, and the work of the Fiscal Crisis and Management Assistance Team (FCMAT). The chapter also discusses the importance of community involvement in managing the budget and the characteristics of ineffective budgeting.

The school district budgeting process involves continuous planning and evaluation. A basic assumption for every district or school is that the budget is a spending *plan*—a plan to accomplish the instructional objectives of the district. A budget is never etched in stone, but typically is modified several times during the fiscal year. A second assumption for school boards, superintendents, and principals is that the solvency of the district must be maintained. Resources should be used as effectively as possible, and the district is obligated to avoid programs and services that it cannot afford. The budget should reflect a strong commitment to maintain the school system's fiscal soundness. Third, school leaders must develop short- and long-range goals and priorities before developing the budget.

Each year, many important decisions are made that impact the budget. Whether to hire or replace staff, what fringe benefits to provide, salary adjustments for employees, new instructional programs, maintenance of facilities, and construction of new schools are just a few of the critical decisions that must be reached in the budget development process.

A good budgeting process provides for input from staff and community in a decentralized mode, while also ensuring that all legal requirements are met. In the past, many districts relied upon an authoritarian mode of budgeting, making all decisions at the superintendent and governing board level. Today, budgets typically begin in a decentralized process, with input from every school and department. This approach has its own failings, however, since limitations on resources mean that many requests cannot be honored.

The State Budget Calendar

California, along with 46 other states, starts the fiscal year in July and ends in June. The exceptions are Alabama and Michigan, which start in October and end in September. New York has an April to March fiscal year, and Texas has September to August. Twenty-one states operate on a biennial budget cycle.

California's budget calendar starts with the governor's presentation of the budget in early January of each year. The state legislator is required to approve the budget by June 15 each year. This constitutional deadline has been met only five times in the last 30 years. The 2010–2011 budget set a record by being 100 days late; in that year the state was forced to pay some of its bills with IOUs. One of the problems was that there was no penalty for the state legislative bodies not meeting the deadline.

Until 2010, California was one of three states that required a two-thirds vote by the legislature to approve the budget. The other two states that still require the super majority are Arkansas and Rhode Island. The super majority requirement was established during the depression, and many attempts were made to change the requirement to a simple majority.

That objective was accomplished in 2010 when California citizens approved Proposition 25. That proposition changed the two-thirds requirement to a simple majority vote rather than the two-thirds. Proposition 25 requires state legislators to forfeit their pay if they do not approve the budget by the June 15th deadline. However, Proposition 25 did not remove the two-thirds vote to raise taxes. The adoption calendar for the state budget is contained in Table 3.

The District Budget Calendar

The first step in developing the budget calendar is to let everyone know the sequence of events and deadlines for decision-making. Timetables vary from district to district, but the basic steps are the same, no matter what time of year the cycle is started. The budget calendar, which should be

Table 3	Typical State Budget Adoption Calendar
January	Governor proposes budget for following year
Late February	Legislative Analyst releases budget analysis
March/April	Legislative Subcommittees hold hearings on the budget
Mid-May	Governor proposes revisions of budget
Late May	Full Committees approve budget; each House adopts a budget
Early June	Conference Committee approves budget; each House adopts the budget
June 15	Constitutional deadline for Legislature to adopt budget
June 30	Constitutional deadline for Governor to sign budget

Table 4	Typical District Budget Adoption Calendar
February	School district develops budget guidelines for next fiscal year
March 15	District serves notice of intent to reduce site-level certificated management personnel (if needed)
March 15	District serves notice of intent to reduce teachers and central office certificated management personnel (if needed)
March 15	Budget worksheets are distributed to program administrators
April 1	District serves notice of intent to reduce classified staff (if needed)
May 1	Employees receive final notice of layoff (if needed)
May 1	Board adopts order to lay off employees
June	Staff presents budget for review by local school board
July 1	District holds public hearing, adopts budget, and files it with the County Office of Education (COE)
August 15	COE approves or disapproves district budget
October 8	COE notifies State Superintendent of Public Instruction (SPI) of district budgets that have been disapproved
October 31	District files first interim with COE; also SPI and State Controller (SC) in case of qualified or negative certification
January 31	District files second interim with COE; also SPI and SC in case of qualified or negative certification

approved by the governing board no later than October or November of each year, is a key document that guides actions of the district throughout the year. The budget calendar should detail dates when budget additions and reductions are reviewed, when worksheets are due in the business office, and when important policy decisions are made. Another feature of the budget calendar is identification of the administrator responsible for each task. Lacking such assignments, tasks to be accomplished by a certain date may be overlooked because no person is accountable for their completion.

The budget calendar should include a deadline for enrollment projections. Accuracy in this projection is fundamental to the accuracy of budget figures. The business officer may project enrollments centrally or may choose to have each principal responsible for estimating school enrollment for the following year. In either case, figures should be reviewed carefully.

It should be recognized that much debate over finances will ensue, even though a district has a budget calendar. With the recent emphasis on restructuring and site-based management, leading to numerous committees and meetings at school sites, many opinions will be expressed and many requests submitted. Given diminishing resources, it sometimes seems that groups and committees are engaged in a futile battle over dwindling assets. Thus, the budget calendar is not a panacea that solves financial problems, but a road map to meet legal requirements and to yield a cohesive plan for managing the district's financial resources. A typical district budget calendar, with timelines for adoption, is set forth in Table 4.

The District Educational Plan

The educational plan is the heart of the budget, reflecting the philosophy and mission of the district. Accomplishing the objectives stated in the plan should be the focus of acquiring funds and allocating expenditures. A successful plan is one that involves each of the stakeholders in its development: students, parents, teachers, staff, administrators, and as many community representatives as possible.

As an example, educational goals in a district's budget might include the following:

- Building instructional capacity
- High quality teaching and leadership

- Learning communities and professional development
- Support for student development
- Schools as centers of communities in partnerships
- Strengthening existing high school programs
- Accountability to support improvement in student achievement

Once the educational plan has been developed and approved by the school board, the next step in the budget process is to determine the district's revenues and expenditures for the next school year. Additional discussion of revenues and expenditures appears in subsequent chapters.

Basic Legal Requirements Governing Budget Development

A significant budget law, AB 1200, was approved by the legislature and signed by the governor in 1991. This law was passed because several California districts had found it necessary to obtain state loans to remain solvent. AB 1200 became effective January 1, 1992. It greatly increased the fiscal authority of county offices of education and of the California Department of Education. Each of these levels of government was authorized to review and monitor local school district budgets. AB 1200 particularly placed greater responsibility on the county office for monitoring, and where necessary, intervening in school district fiscal matters. The law established a system of checks and balances to provide each board of education and the administration with early awareness of potential financial problems. It was also designed to facilitate assistance from the county level to local districts.

Specifically, AB 1200

- changed the previous budget adoption process and timelines
- expanded the definition of solvency by addressing a district's ability to meet multi-year, and not just current year, commitments
- identified new local requirements to be met before ratification of collective bargaining agreements
- provided a new process to be followed if budgets are disapproved by the county superintendent of schools
- established stern consequences for failure to meet the above provisions

School districts must end the year with a balanced budget. To ensure this condition, they are required to set aside a specified percent of the budget for economic uncertainties. The percentage depends upon students in attendance.

Attendance	Required Set-Aside
300 or less	5% or $50,000
300 to 1,000	4% or $50,000
1,001 to 30,000	3%
30,001 to 400,000	2%
400,001 or more (Los Angeles)	1%

State Emergency Loans and AB 2756

A district that is unable to meet the annual financial obligation may have no other recourse than to petition the state for an emergency loan. As a condition of acceptance of the loan, the state superintendent appoints an administrator or trustee to control, monitor, and review the operation of the district. A major responsibility of this administrator is to assist the district in developing a five-year recovery plan.

About 35 school districts in California have received state loans, including Berkeley, Oakland, West Contra Costa, West Covina, Coachella, and Compton. Between 2001 and 2017, five districts had emergency loans: Inglewood Unified, South Monterey County, Vallejo City Unified, Oakland Unified, and Compton Unified. The loans ranged from $13,000,000 to $100,000,000 (CDE, 2017).

In light of this escalation of fiscal emergencies in school districts, AB 2756 was passed and signed in June 2004. As summarized by the Legislative Counsel, this legislation tightened oversight of district fiscal management as follows:

- Standards and criteria for district budget development are to be updated.
- The County Superintendent of Schools must notify the California Board of Accountancy should it determine that a district audit was not appropriately conducted.
- County oversight is strengthened and backed by the possibility of the Superintendent of Public Instruction stepping into the role of the county office.
- Both districts and county offices must comply with added requirements in reviewing collective bargaining agreements, although the county's time limit for this review is extended from six to ten working days.

The bill was declared an urgency statute and took effect immediately.

Fiscal Crisis and Management Assistance Team (FCMAT)

An additional component of Assembly Bill 1200 was the requirement that the state develop an agency designed to assist districts with their financial and management responsibilities The assembly bill specified that one county office of education would be selected to administer the program. The Kern County Superintendent of Schools was chosen for this task. In the 20 plus years of FCMAT's existence, it has performed many services for districts. For example:

- FCMAT has assisted more than 1000 school districts and county offices with financial management and issues.
- FCMAT has organized and presented dozens of staff development programs.
- FCMAT manages a website that provides resources (including state budget development software) for school districts and county offices of education. The Website is located at http://www.fcmat.org
- FCMAT provides management studies for districts and county offices.
- When a county office disapproves a district's annual budget, the county office may request that FCMAT assist the district in achieving fiscal stability.

Under AB 2756, FCMAT continues to play a crucial role with respect to insolvent districts. Its ability to review financial and administrative operations was expanded beyond county offices to include school districts and charter schools.

Interim Financial Reports

Interim financial reports have been required for the past several years. The state requires that boards certify in October and again in January that their finances are in good shape. However, AB 1200 gives substantial new authority to the county superintendent of schools when reviewing these reports. Three classes of certification were established:

- **Positive Certification**—This certification means that the district has sufficient resources to meet its financial obligations for the current fiscal year and two years subsequent.

- **Qualified Certification**—This certification means that the district may have sufficient resources to meet its financial obligations for the current fiscal year and two years subsequent.

- **Negative Certification**—This certification means that the district does not have the resources to meet its financial obligations for the remainder of the fiscal year or the subsequent fiscal year.

These reports are submitted to the county superintendent, with negative reports sent to the Office of the State Controller and the State Superintendent of Public Instruction. When a district certifies a negative financial report, the county superintendent has authority to develop and adopt a budget for the district. The county superintendent also may rescind any financial action that is inconsistent with that budget. Districts with a qualified or negative certification may not issue certificates of participation, tax anticipation notes, revenue bonds, or any other debt instrument not requiring voter approval.

The California Department of Education (CDE, 2014) reported that 30 California districts filed a negative or qualified certification in 2013. That number was an improvement from a year earlier when 92 districts reported financial trouble.

Fiscal Advisors

Under AB 1200 the county superintendent may assign fiscal advisors to a district that has been determined unable to meet its financial obligations. The communication to the district from the county office begins with a meeting between a county staff member and the district superintendent and business staff. After this discussion, the committee meets with the district governing board. Districts that are unable to avoid fiscal insolvency may receive an emergency state apportionment, but only as a last resort. When this action is taken, the state superintendent appoints a trustee to supervise the district. The trustee reports directly to the state superintendent until the loan is repaid.

Characteristics of Ineffective Budgeting

The late Stan Oswalt, a former California superintendent and a state-appointed fiscal advisor, pointed out fiscal red flags that are as relevant today as when he shared them more than two decades ago. First, Oswalt described five characteristics of ineffective budgeting:

- **Ineffective estimations of ending balances**—Accounts receivable are overestimated, and accounts payable are underestimated.

- **Ineffective budget development**—Federal, state, and local income are overestimated, and expenditures are underestimated. In addition, reserves for economic uncertainties are inadequate.

- **Ineffective budget monitoring and reporting**—The budget is not adjusted as revenues are reduced. Adequate information for management decisions is not made available, and planned expenditures are not encumbered. Further, encroachment of restricted programs on the General Fund is not reduced.

- **Ineffective attendance accounting**—Attendance is not projected accurately, and adjustments are not made for inaccurate reporting.

- **Ineffective personnel practices**—The staff of the business or personnel office fail to maintain adequate personnel records. Multi-year personnel contracts exist, but precise cost of positions is not calculated.

In addition to the characteristics of ineffective budgeting, Oswalt also identified several danger signals that may precede financial insolvency:

- **Cash flow problems**—Districts headed for financial problems often have need to borrow from other sources before they turn to the state. When the borrowing is based on unrealistic revenue or expenditure projections, the district runs out of cash.

- **Small beginning and ending balances**—Without an adequate beginning and ending balance, the district greatly reduces its ability to cope with unforeseen circumstances.

- **Unrealistic collective bargaining contracts**—This factor led to near insolvency in Los Angeles Unified School District. As a result of a strike, certificated employees were granted a 24% raise over a three-year period. When the COLA from the state was significantly less than the pay increase, the district found itself in a very difficult financial situation. Multi-year contracts without ties to revenues or expenditures and without a re-opener pose great financial danger to a district.

- **Turnover in administration**—Turnover in key positions such as superintendent, chief business official, or director of accounting affects consistency of management in a district. Oswalt states that a turnover rate of more than three chief business officials and/or superintendents in five years may indicate a financial problem.

- **Lack of experience in key personnel**—The background and experience of the superintendent and chief business official and other key people in the business office can have a significant effect on the successful financial operation of the district.

- **Lax internal controls**—If clear and concise controls are not in place, unwise decisions may be made about expenditures.

- **Inadequate financial review**—Financial reports must be frequent and reliable if the school board and superintendent are to make quality decisions. Financial reports should be presented in an open session of the board of education and should be in writing, never just verbal.

- **Internal political straggles**—Political struggles make it difficult for strong, positive, and continuing leadership to exist. Board members assuming the role of the superintendent or other key administrative personnel may signal serious problems.

- **Enrollment decline**—It is often difficult for a district to adjust to declining enrollment. School board members and the superintendent may be reluctant to make the hard decisions to reduce staff and programs. Closure of schools, which may be needed in the face of declining enrollment, may also be a political decision that puts the district at financial risk (Oswalt, 1992).

Community and Individual School Participation

Because of the current emphasis upon the concept of restructuring, much effort is given to beginning budget discussions at school sites. Actually, districts that are successful in implementing restructuring employ both decentralized and centralized budgeting procedures.

School Site Decentralization

Committees are typically formed at the school site to discuss all budget policies related to that site. These discussions may address topics ranging from staffing to use of the copy machine. Most often, the school principal forms these committees and participates in committee discussions and recommendations. He or she should be influential in reviewing community and staff recommendations and deciding which may be useful and which not.

Inevitably, some suggestions will conflict with policies imposed by central office budgeting decisions. For example, teachers might like a class ratio of 20:1, or perhaps discretionary use of all lottery funds. However, because of finite resources, restructuring committees must realize at the start that certain desires at the school site cannot be fulfilled. Nevertheless, the discussions and debate are, in and of themselves, a valuable tool for building teamsmanship. In addition, one of the main tenets of site-based management is the formation of "responsible parties." Planning for change within inevitable constraints, even though some actions cannot be accomplished at once, helps that responsibility to mature.

Centralized Budgeting Mode

Even in a centralized budgeting mode, budget sheets and computer printouts are typically distributed to each school principal and collected by the business staff to be included in the budget. Site income may be centrally determined, but distribution across expenditure categories is somewhat flexible. In any case, the governing board has the final decision in structuring the school district budget, even though the board may solicit input from the superintendent and staff.

SUMMARY

The school district budget serves as a blueprint or master plan for the district. It should be a document that clearly establishes priorities for the district. A successful budget requires skill and expertise on the part of the business staff who project revenues and expenditures. Outstanding leadership and communication skills also are required by the board, superintendent, and principals as they involve staff, parents, and the community in developing this document.

AB 1200 and AB 2756 are a mandate to school districts that unwise or imprudent financial decisions leading toward insolvency will not be tolerated. The law clearly and forcefully takes authority away from local boards who endanger the solvency of public schools.

Budgeting is a political, as well as rational, issue. The district budget is a spending *plan*. It establishes the priorities and objectives of a district and a community. A cursory examination of a district's budget reveals the priorities of the district. What, for example, is the level of support for school athletics—or for music? What attention is paid to landscaping and maintenance of facilities? What is the level of support for the college preparatory curriculum and the vocational education program? Questions like these reflect a community's commitment to programs and priorities.

In most districts the process of budget development calls for participation by many groups in the district. The governing board typically listens to all groups and makes decisions by balancing their beliefs against the fiscal constraints imposed upon them.

KEY TERMS

AB 1200

AB 2756

District budget calendar

Enrollment projections

FCMAT

Interim financial reports

Legislative Analyst

Spending plan

State budget calendar

Discussion/Essay Questions

1. The district budget is a plan for accomplishing the educational objectives of the district. Discuss three necessary budget priorities for accomplishing this objective.

2. Although the state legislature is required to submit a budget to the governor by June 15, this requirement is rarely met. Discuss major reasons for failure of the legislature to meet this deadline and suggest remedies to ensure compliance.

3. The district budget calendar is a management plan to ensure development of an optimum budget. Discuss the major components that should be included in a successful budget calendar.

4. All California districts are required to submit two interim financial reports each year to the County Superintendent of Schools. The County Superintendent has authority to establish one of three certifications for each interim report. Discuss the three certifications and the significance of each.

School District Revenue

I think children should have the first call on the budget.

(Arnold Schwarzenegger, Governor of California—interview with Matt Lauer of NBC)

Introduction

Although education is a function of the state, this responsibility has been delegated to local school districts. Because many local districts have difficulty generating and managing their finances, states are assuming greater financial responsibility for schools. With this responsibility comes greater control over the schools. This trend is clearly exemplified in California, as shown in the previous chapters. In particular, Proposition 13, which moved the major source of school district revenue to the state level, and AB 1200, which intensified county and state oversight of school district finance, have weakened fiscal autonomy at the district level while shifting fiscal control to county and state government.

For the first time in 40 years, the funding formula for schools was drastically changed in 2013. The new formula is called Local Control Funding Formula (LCFF). This change is designed to give school districts an unprecedented level of local control. The two major goals of LCFF are to provide more money to school districts, which have a greater number of high-needs students, and to give school districts more authority on how to spend their education dollars. This new funding formula is discussed in greater detail later in this chapter.

It has also been suggested that the vehicle by which funds flow to students may be flawed. Many citizens and educators believe that each school site should be empowered to collect monies directly from local taxpayers or the state. The school could use this money to purchase support from the district or the county, much as a private company might do.

It has also been suggested that the school board turn most control over to local sites, meeting only two to three times per year to establish broad policies for the schools.

All California school districts receive funds from state, local, and federal sources. Some of these funds are designated for specific purposes, while other monies have no strings attached. The state provides nearly 4/5 of the total monies for K–12 education. Consequently, the state's major revenue sources—sales tax and personal income tax—are key elements in the overall support of public education. In California, the federal government provides nearly 13% of the funds for K–12 education; the remainder comes from state and local sources (Ed-Data, 2011).

Taxes

Individuals receive income from a variety of sources: employment, investments, inheritance, and so on. Companies receive income from manufacturing and selling products or services. Governmental agencies are primarily dependent on taxes as a source of revenue. Some form of taxation is perhaps as old as human communication. It is not too difficult to imagine the cave man demanding three animal furs for the right to share his cave with another individual. While the contribution of furs does not fit the modern definition of a tax, it has some of the essential elements.

Taxes are referred to in early historical documents, including the Bible. Terms in the Old Testament refer to taxes as "tributes," "conscription," "forced labor," and "tolls." They were levied as customs taxes, poll taxes, and on property and produce. Exodus 30:11–16 speaks of a tax of a half shekel per person, whether rich or poor. In the New Testament (Matthew 22:15–22) Jesus, when asked about paying taxes to Rome, gave the oft-quoted response, "Give to Caesar what is Caesar's, and to God what is God's" (Metzger & Coogan, 1993). The *Columbia Encyclopedia* (2004) defines "taxation" as a "system used by governments to obtain money from people and organizations," the revenue being "used by the government to support itself and to provide public services." The encyclopedia notes that taxation is compulsory.

Citizens have always had a love/hate relationship with taxes. Individuals greatly enjoy the benefits of services provided by taxes, e.g., schools, roads, police and fire protection, and health services. However, history is replete with citizens refusing to pay taxes. Often this refusal has led to civil unrest or even war, as in the case of Americans rebelling against England with the cry, "No taxation without representation."

One can almost hear the collective groans on April 15 when it is pay-up time for the national income tax or in April and December, when property taxes fall due. Perhaps the strongest support for a tax comes when the individual does not have to pay it. And yet, Americans have a good track record for supporting all levels of government by paying their taxes in general assent to Benjamin Franklin's assertion that nothing is more certain than death and taxes.

Classification of Taxes

Taxes are generally classified as proportional, progressive, and regressive. Proportional taxes occur when one taxpayer's percentage is the same as that of all other taxpayers, regardless of income. A progressive tax means that the percentage increases as the individual's income become higher. Finally, a tax is called "regressive" if an individual with a higher income pays a lower percentage than someone with a smaller income.

- **Proportional Tax**—Suppose that three individuals earn $30,000, $40,000, and $50,000 and they pay $3,000, $4,000, and $5,000 in taxes, respectively. Each individual is paying 10% of income for taxes. That exemplifies the proportional tax. Generally, property taxes are proportional taxes. The tax is based on the assessed value of the home and property, and all owners pay the same percentage of the value. As discussed in Chapter 2, this is not always the case in California.

- **Progressive Tax**—If the above individuals were paying $3,000, 8,000, and $15,000, the tax would be classified as progressive. These taxpayers are assessed 10%, 20%, and 30%, respectively. Examples of a progressive tax are the state income tax in California and the national income tax. The greater one's salary, the greater the percentage of taxes.

- **Regressive Tax**—If the same individuals were paying $3,000, $2,000, and $1,000, respectively, the tax would be classified as regressive. In some instances the sales tax operates as a regressive tax, as a buyer with low income is paying proportionally higher taxes out of disposable income than a wealthier person. For example, if food and other necessities are subject to sales tax, the tax could be regressive. In an attempt to avoid this effect, California does not place sales tax on food. The structure of sales tax greatly varies from state to state.

Consumption Taxes

Consumption taxes are taxes based on spending, rather than income. An example of such a tax is the state sales tax. Another form of consumption tax is the value-added tax, or VAT, which is essentially a national sales tax. The United States does not have a VAT, although this type of taxation has received considerable discussion and attention during the past decade. A VAT would be imposed at each stage of production, from obtaining the raw material to manufacturing and retail sale. The VAT is common in industrialized countries around the world.

The term "consumption tax" is most frequently used to describe excise taxes on specific goods and services. Examples include liquors, tobacco, gasoline, hotel rooms, fine jewelry, and other luxury goods. An energy tax is also based on consumption; on the average, state and federal gasoline taxes add about 37 cents to the price of a gallon of unleaded gasoline.

The advantage of a consumption tax is that a small rate can raise enormous amounts of money. An additional tax of five cents per gallon on gasoline would generate more than $5 billion a year in federal revenue. A second benefit of such a tax is that as the economy improves, governments automatically benefit without having to pass new taxes. Also, raising so-called "sin taxes" on items such as tobacco and alcohol is easier to sell to voters than hiking income or property taxes. Moreover, such a tax is easily and efficiently collected through existing systems: a cash register, gasoline pump, or monthly utility bills.

About 17 percent of U.S. tax revenue is raised from consumption taxes—primarily sales and excise taxes. Consumption taxes are far more important to the European Community nations, which on average obtain more than 30 percent of total tax revenue from such taxes. For example, CNN (2017) reported in 2017, the price per U.S. gallon of unleaded premium gasoline was more than $5.00 dollars in Italy, Germany, France, and the United Kingdom, compared to less than $4.00 in the United States. Almost all of the disparity is related to fuel tax.

A major disadvantage of a consumption tax is that it is regressive. A tax on necessities penalizes the poor and middle classes more than the rich. A second problem is that consumption tax revenues drop as an economy slows, just when government services are needed most.

Determining District Income

When the chief financial officer of a school district faces the task of projecting income, he or she must keep in mind that California schools are highly dependent on funding from the state. In good economic times the schools share in the good news. However, the reverse is also true; when the economy of California turns south as it did in 2008, the state had a difficult time in balancing its budget, and consequently so did education. The reduction in state funds for schools continued through the proposed budget for 2012–2013.

As stated earlier, the state provides the major share of funding for public education. This income is largely derived from the state personal income tax, sales tax, and corporation tax. For example, in the 2017-2018 state budget, the personal income tax represented 71 percent of revenue, followed by sales tax at 20 percent, and corporation tax at seven percent. Other state revenue comes from highway use taxes, motor vehicle taxes, insurance taxes, alcoholic beverage taxes, and cigarette taxes (LAO, 2017).

A review of the source of state income illustrates how uncertain and difficult it is to estimate income. If the state's economy declines, corporations make less money and pay fewer taxes. In addition, the corporations may lay off employees or not grant pay increases, which results in citizens paying less income taxes. With less disposable income, purchases are postponed or delayed, which results in less income from sales tax. It is the domino effect, with each source of income depending on another, and when one falls, it affects the total structure.

Revenue Estimation for the Next Year

A budget calendar provides a blueprint for timing certain reports and projections. Usually by December or January of each school year, the business office has received sufficient fiscal information about the subsequent year's income to begin the process of revenue estimation. These are the best months in which to begin the tough job of estimating the following year's income.

The CBO must rely on two primary sources of information that are available in December. One source is the monthly expenditure reports that have been generated for the first six months of the fiscal year. The second source of information is reports of actual student attendance. These two reports help determine trends from which to project the all-important ending balance for the current year and the all-important enrollment for the subsequent year.

Local Control Funding Formula (LCFF)

In 2013, California's Governor Brown signed a new funding formula for California schools. The governor is a strong supporter of giving local districts more power on how education dollars are spent rather than financial decisions made at the state. This change in how schools are funded is the first major change since Proposition 13 was approved in 1978.

The new funding law ended the old system of "revenue-limits." Under "revenue-limits," districts received an amount per student, plus categorical aid. This amount was based on complex historical formulas with similar districts receiving a very different amount per student.

A major goal of LCFF is to include parents, community members, teachers, staff, and students in making decisions of how dollars are spent. The premises of the law are as follows:

- LCFF will make California school funding more equitable.
- A large share of K-12 students are English learners and cost more to educate.

- A large number of students come from low-income families and cost more to educate.
- The old formula—revenue limits—did not reflect the cost of educating different students.
- LCFF provides a base grant for all students and additional funds for the above-mentioned students.
- LCFF allocates resources to school districts, charter schools, and county offices of education based on student needs.
- LCFF provides school districts with greater authority over the use of resources.
- LCFF requires each district and charter school to adopt a local accountability plan and allocate spending sufficient to implement the plan.
- LCFF excludes funds from parcel taxes, funds for special education, the After School and Safety Program, transportation, and child nutrition.
- LCFF excludes all federal dollars.

The LCFF formula has been included in district budgets in each year since 2013-2014. Full funding will be phased in over an eight-year period with final implementation in 2020-2021. Until full funding is reached, districts will receive funds each year based on student attendance and the percentage of a district's students who are designated as low-income, English learners, and foster youth.

Under the LCFF, most state categorical programs are eliminated and school districts receive funding based on the demographic profile of district students. Districts will be funded the same amount as in the past with adjustments for the number of students from low-income families, English learners, and foster youth. The LCFF system establishes a funding target for each district to reach during the next eight years. The funding target is unique to each district depending on student demographics and funding designed to reach the district's objective.

Local Control Accountability Plan (LCAP)

LCAP is the accountability component of the LCFF process. Starting in 2014–2015, each school district is required to create a three-year plan aligned to the district budget. The plan must describe the school district's overall vision for students, annual goals, and the specific actions the district will take to achieve the goals. The plan is not difficult to develop. However, it does require a great deal of time and effort to gather input from a wide array of stakeholders. Districts will receive funding specifically aimed to support services for students classified as low-income, English learners, and foster youth.

Monthly Expenditure Reports

It is the responsibility of the business office to monitor the expenditure reports each month. Salaries and benefits are particularly important: Now that the district has completed six months of the fiscal year, are salaries and benefit expenditures approximately 50% of what was budgeted in these categories? If expenditures exceed 50%, adjustments may be required for that category. A particularly critical area is the amount expended for utilities. A couple of percentage points over budgeted amounts for electricity can leave a large gap in a district's ending balance.

The CBO should also check the last six months of the preceding year for large annual payments that may come due during that time. This avoids the error of assuming that large amounts unspent at mid-year are available for other purposes.

Enrollment Projections

Enrollment projections are significant, not only because they indicate income, but also because they determine classroom usage and the number of teaching positions needed. All districts should prepare five- to ten-year projections for enrollment, income, and expenditures. Even if the income formula changes, having a plan that can be adjusted is much better than having no plan at all. Long-range projections accustom the staff to long-range planning.

Another figure of interest is sometimes called the "birth-to-kindergarten survival rate." This rate shows the relationship between the number of children born within a district and the number that, as young families move in or out of the area, can be expected to enroll in kindergarten five years hence. Such a prediction can help avoid unwanted surprises.

Enrollment projections are so critical that many districts involve district staff and principals in projecting the enrollment for the next year. Other districts employ consultants who specialize in providing this information. In addition, some districts rely on community organizations, e.g., realtors, developers, and community service agencies, to assist in projecting new housing that is expected within the district.

One cannot overemphasize the importance of accurate and reliable student enrollment projections for the next school year. For example, a school that over-projects enrollment by 60 students will receive approximately $420,000 (60 · $7,000 income per student) less revenue than had been anticipated. If we assume two teachers are already under contract for the 60 students at a cost of $50,000 each, the combined loss of revenue and committed expenditures may exceed half a million dollars.

Actual-Attendance Calculation

Prior to the 1998–99 school year, all California school districts and county offices received state dollars for every day that a student actually attended class. Districts also received funds for absences that were excused, usually for illness. Since fall, 1998, however, districts have been funded only for days students are actually in class. This procedure is known as "actual attendance accounting." The objective of making the change was to give districts an incentive to maximize student attendance and to decrease absences for any cause.

Most districts base their revenue projections on a 97% to 98% percent attendance rate or on average actual daily attendance (ADA). Unfortunately, there is a wide discrepancy among districts in their ADA rate. As little as 1% difference in attendance may translate into a very large sum of money. For example, let us assume that a district has an enrollment of 10,000 students and a base revenue of $7,000 per student. If all students had perfect attendance, the income would be $70,000,000. If the actual attendance averages only 98%—a 2% loss in attendance—the corresponding revenue loss comes to $1,400,000.

In 2009–2010, KPBS, a San Diego news station, reported that public schools in San Diego County lost $102 million in state funding because of absences. At Ramona Unified, 473 chronically absent students cost the district $35,567.00. Twenty-seven students missed 35% of the school days in that year. Two students were absent more than 100 days (KPBS, 2011).

Cost of Living Adjustment (COLA)

Proposition 98 provides an overall minimum allocation to K–12 education of 40% of state revenues, but the COLA is an increased amount per ADA that is apportioned over and above the Proposition 98 minimum. Current law ties COLAs to various indices of inflation, although different amounts are appropriated in some years.

In most years, increases from one percent to four percent are identified as COLA in the Governor's budget. The COLA is used in a formula with ADA to determine the amount of each district's total revenue limit, which is the largest income assigned to each district. Over the past four decades, districts have received a COLA in every year except 1982 and three years in the early 1990s.

Categorical Revenue

As discussed earlier in this chapter, under the LCFF, most state categorical programs are eliminated and school districts receive funding based on the demographic profile of district students. Districts will have the ability to decide to fund or not to fund previous categorical programs, i.e., gifted and talented, deferred maintenance, and driver training. However, the district will budget revenue for expenditures that are still funded, i.e., After School Program, transportation, and all federal programs.

Special Education Income

As the CBO constructs the budget, a determination of revenues for special education must be calculated. Special education funds are allocated from various sources, including federal, state, and local aid. Special education includes a wide variety of programs such as Designated Instructional Services, Resource Specialists, Special Day Classes, placement in non-public facilities, and state special education schools.

Lottery Funds

The California State Lottery Act (Proposition 37) was approved by the voters in 1984 and implemented by the state legislature in 1985. The Lottery Act states that the purpose of the California lottery is to generate funding to supplement the public education budget to the extent of at least 34% of sales. The funds are distributed to several sectors of public education, including K–12 school districts, community colleges, and county offices of education.

The lottery was touted to the public as a great benefit to schools. When advocates of the lottery were attempting to persuade California voters to approve its passage, television commercials showed students using computers and taking special field trips paid for with lottery funds. However, from a high point of $176 in 1998–1999, the amount has leveled at about $130–157 per pupil (see Figure 2).

Typically, public education has received 36-39 percent of proceeds, the larger percentage as the result of savings in administration and unclaimed prizes. Of lottery proceeds, 50% is returned to players as prizes, and 16% is used to administer the lottery. The original proposition stipulated that all unclaimed jackpots were to be returned to public education.

Most unclaimed winnings have been small amounts. However, over the years, the unclaimed prize money has added up. As of 2015 more than $800 million in unclaimed prizes have been awarded to schools (California Lottery, 2017).

Despite these dramatic figures, lottery funds have not greatly contributed to financing education. In reality, the allocation translates to less than 2% of a school district's general fund budget. This amount is much below that perceived by the public. Moreover, because quarterly payments of lottery funds have varied widely, most business managers budget lottery income in a very conservative fashion.

Lottery funds may be spent for any purpose except construction or purchase of buildings. A minor limitation was added in March of 2000, when California voters approved Proposition 20.

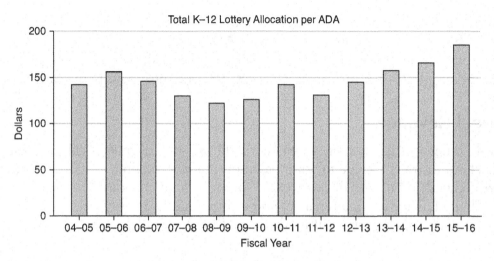

Figure 2 **California State Lottery**
SOURCE: California State Lottery

This provision requires that half of the annual increase in funds beyond the 1997–98 year be spent on instructional materials.

More than one billion dollars in lottery funds goes to California public schools each year. The money is used to fund professional development, special programs, and the purchase of instructional materials (California Lottery, 2017).

Other Sources of Revenue

Other sources of local funds include user fees, interest income, sale and lease of property, cafeteria fees, and library fines. Districts may form partnerships with other governmental agencies to provide fee-supported programs at school sites. For example, forming a partnership with the local recreation department to provide swimming or other recreational activities is a common practice.

School districts are prohibited from charging students or their parents for books or supplies. However, after several court challenges, the California Supreme Court ruled in 1992 that a district may charge for student transportation. Still, districts may not charge for transporting special education students or for student participation in school programs such as athletics.

Donations

Donations are also sources of income in many districts. Foundations and corporations frequently make grants directly to school districts for special programs. Many companies also encourage their employees to volunteer in schools.

Revenue Accounts

The Bible for school district accounts is the *California State School Accounting Manual*. It was revised in 2016. It can be ordered from the California Department of Education. All California school districts are required to record their financial affairs in compliance with the definitions, instructions, and procedures published in the manual. The reports provide information to the school board, administration, teachers, and the public to track income and expenditures.

SUMMARY

For the first time in 40 years, the funding formula for schools was drastically changed in 2013. The new formula is called Local Control Funding Formula (LCFF). This change is designed to give school districts an unprecedented level of local control. The two major goals of LCFF are to provide more money to school districts, which have a greater number of high-needs students, and to give school districts more authority on how to spend their education dollars.

In 2013, California's Governor Brown signed a new funding formula for California schools. The governor is a strong supporter of giving local districts more power on how education dollars are spent, rather than financial decisions made at the state. This change in how schools are funded is the first major change since Proposition 13 was approved in 1978.

Local Control Accountability Plan (LCAP) is the accountability component of the LCFF process. Starting in 2014–2015, each school district is required to create a three-year plan aligned to the district budget. The plan must describe the school district's overall vision for students, annual goals, and the specific actions the district will take to achieve the goals.

All California school districts receive funds from state, local, and federal sources. The state provides nearly two-thirds of the total monies for K-12. Districts depend on other sources for the balance of income. Districts are exploring a variety of options to provide additional revenue, such as developer fees, parcel taxes, and charging fees for services. Donations are also a source of income in many districts. Foundations and corporations frequently make grants directly to school districts for special programs. Many school districts have a major goal of improving student attendance, which will result in improved student achievement and income for the district.

KEY TERMS

ADA	Progressive tax
Business tax	Property tax
COLA	Proportional tax
Consumption tax	Regressive tax
Income tax	Sales tax
Local Control Accountability Plan (LCAP)	Sin tax
Local Control Funding Formula (LCFF)	User fees
Partnerships	Value-added tax

Discussion/Essay Questions

1. The three major sources of revenue for California school districts are the state income tax, state sales tax, and property tax. What are the advantages and disadvantages of each of these sources of government income?

2. The United States does not currently have a value-added tax (VAT). What are the major arguments for and against this form of taxation?

3. "Sin taxes" are increasingly popular with federal and state legislatures. Give an example of a "sin tax" and discuss the pros and cons of this form of taxation.

4. Nearly all federal monies allocated for public education are "categorical." Explain this term and give examples of federal categorical aid to school districts. What is the rationale for each?

Program Budgeting and Expenditures Accounting

Program Budgeting is not a panacea. It is not a substitute for the experience, intuition, and judgement of educational planners.

(John Ray, Walter Hack, and I. Carl Candoli, School Business Administration)

Introduction

Districts concerned with the costs of operating diverse programs utilize program budgeting. This system allocates income and expenditures to specific cost centers. Districts use a system of account codes, required by the California Department of Education, to identify specific costs by program or department. As described later in this chapter, the codes incorporate six elements: fund/group, resource, project year, goal, function, and object. Specific accounting details for program budgeting, including revenue and expenditures codes, are found in the latest edition of the *California School Accounting Manual,* from which much of the material in this chapter is selected. The manual may be ordered in hard copy from the California Department of Education or obtained online at http://www.cde.ca.gov/fg/ac/sa/

Typically, a district maintains a chart of accounts to interpret the financial reports of the district. For example, to track costs of the gifted and talented program in a district over a three-year period, program budgeting would enable one to collect all program income and expenditure figures for this span of time. Typically, school districts tie goals and objectives to program budgets, being careful to analyze the cost of achieving agreed-upon objectives.

Program budgeting is designed to provide school district decision-makers, the public, and the legislature with detailed information about the services and benefits purchased by a district. Program budgeting assumes that each program will be assessed periodically to determine its usefulness and effectiveness. To this end, program expenditures are evaluated in conjunction with the district's goals and objectives. This information assists the superintendent and governing board to decide whether to eliminate, reduce, or increase the funding of a particular program.

There are four types of program budgeting: incremental or historical; planning, programming, budgeting; zero-based; and site-based. Incremental or historical budgeting has the longest track record for building budgets in the public and private sector. Budget reformers' attempts to institute new types of program budgeting in public school systems have met with but partial success.

Incremental or Historical Budgeting

The starting point in incremental budgeting is the prior year budget. The process calls for increasing or decreasing the previous year's allocation for each budget item by a percentage. Decisions are made for each existing line item, either to add or subtract dollars, to carry the item forward unchanged, or to delete it entirely. The vast bulk of expenditures continue year after year, budget cycle after budget cycle. Under this system, allocations change very little from year to year.

The rationale for incremental budgeting is that the major portion of a district's budget is allocated to salaries and benefits. District decision-makers feel they have little latitude for significant changes in other expenditures. An advantage of the incremental approach is its relative simplicity. Certain "fixed" costs—such as utilities, insurance, and supplies—are easily adjusted. Salaries and benefits can be projected and calculated. This system also creates less anxiety on the part of employees, who may fear that more detailed budget scrutiny could result in discontinuance of a particular program. The major disadvantage to incremental budgeting is that it may not respond to changing district needs. As a consequence, existing programs may continue beyond their usefulness and, unless new funds or resources become available, institution of new programs is likely to be difficult.

Planning-Programming-Budgeting System (PPBS)

In the 1960s, Robert McNamara, then Secretary of Defense, introduced a systems analysis approach at the Defense Department. His hope was this system would provide decision-makers with more reliable information in the budgeting process. This *planning-programming-budgeting system* became known as PPBS. McNamara, who had been an executive at Ford Motor Company, believed that PPBS would provide more precise evaluation of program outcomes. The success of the process prompted other government departments to institute similar planning techniques.

PPBS is a centralized budgeting system. In this approach, goals are established at the district level, after which budget development proceeds downward to departments and school sites. The primary objective of PPBS is to provide decision-makers with more complete, accurate, and objective information for planning educational programs and for choosing among alternatives in spending funds to achieve educational objectives. Program budgeting assumes that each program, or at least a significant portion of programs, will be assessed periodically to determine their usefulness and effectiveness. Programs that are judged as not meeting agreed-upon objectives would then be improved or eliminated.

An early criticism of PPBS was a felt lack of evaluation in the system. Consequently, evaluation was added, making the system PPBES. The Association of School Business Officials attempted to make the system more compatible with school district budgeting practices and renamed it ERMD (Educational Resource Management Division).

The major advantage of PPBS lies in providing a way to measure limited resources against the objectives of the district and subsequently to retain and reject programs that are or are not in concert with objectives. In addition, PPBS fosters a long-term view by extending the planning period and duration of program budgeting to five or more years. A major disadvantage of this system is the enormous amount of data that must be collected and the time-consuming task of analyzing the data. A second disadvantage in the system is that it is top-down, driven by major objectives established at the district board level.

Zero-Based Budgeting (ZBB)

Arthur Burns, former chairman of the Federal Reserve Board, is generally credited with the first public use of the term zero-based budgeting (ZBB); that was in 1969. However, the concept of ZBB was actually initiated by Peter A. Phyrr, a manager at Texas Instruments. Rather than continue the allocation of funds for each program year after year, Texas Instruments decided to begin each year from ground zero. The objective was to review all programs, and thus to improve allocations for the subsequent year. This type of budgeting received additional attention in 1979, when President Carter issued an executive order directing each federal agency to submit budget requests following the ZBB format.

In contrast to PPBS, zero-based budgeting builds from the bottom up. The basic concept of ZBB is that all administrators reassess their programs annually. The one cardinal principle for ZBB is that nothing is sacred. Every program, if it is to receive funding, must be justified during each budget development cycle. Budget requests are ranked and justified by the principal or supervisor and forwarded to the next level. The administrator is asked to provide justification for the financial resources requested to meet program goals. Final decisions are made by the school board and superintendent. The objective of ZBB is to force a rigorous evaluation of all programs. Once each program has been subjected to the evaluation procedure, it may be continued, discontinued, or modified—with appropriate allocation of resources.

There are several advantages to this type of budgeting, including involvement of teachers and staff members, the required annual evaluation of all programs, and the development of priorities with alternatives. As with PPBS, critics of ZBB point to the great amount of paperwork involved in the process and the need for more administrative time in the preparation of the budget. Thus, a disadvantage is the feeling that the system is too complicated and impractical for school districts. Prior commitments created by collective bargaining contracts, teacher tenure, and funds already earmarked for school construction also make true zero-based budgeting very difficult for districts.

Site-Based Budgeting (SBB)

School principals and teachers have always had some discretion over particular elements of the school budget. Such items have included school supplies, textbooks, and—to a limited extent—expenditures for capital equipment. The recent trend, however, is to allow greater discretion in budget development, including such categories as staffing and capital improvements, to decision-makers at the school site.

California's new funding formula, Local Control Funding Formula (LCFF), and the accountability requirement, Local Control Accountability Plan (LCAP), mandates greater involvement of parents, teachers, and students in deciding how funds are spent. Therefore, it is likely that Site-Based Budgeting will be utilized to a greater extent than ever.

This new state formula eliminates most categorical funds and adds others aligned to students' needs. The San Francisco School District developed a guide to assist stakeholders in this process. The guide, Site-Based Budget Development, is an excellent source for school districts that lack experience in that area.

Site-based budgeting (SBB) is a practice wherein teachers, staff, community members, and administrators develop the budget at the school site. SBB has as its primary objective to match student needs to available resources. It places decision-making at the level nearest students, in the hands of teachers and staff who will implement the decisions. For example, schools in such a district may have latitude to purchase the services of two teacher aides in place of one certificated teacher or to employ a music specialist rather than a reading teacher. In California, charter schools and restructuring are two programs designed to place greater authority at the site level, in the hands of the principal, staff, and community members. School-level decision-makers, usually the principal assisted by a school advisory council of teachers and parents, decide on allocation of resources.

SBB appears to have several advantages. It can provide site participants greater latitude in matching local needs and objectives with available resources. In addition, it may improve morale and motivation of staff and community members at the local school. By its very nature, decentralized budgeting forces wider participation in program planning. Acknowledging the unique culture of each particular school and staff, SBB brings together the principal, teachers, staff, community members, and—in secondary schools, at least—students to develop an improved educational program for their school. It tends to allow greater innovation in programs than does a centralized budgeting process.

Critics of SBB charge that it may compartmentalize education in the community. Each school may become independent of the district and settle for a narrow focus of goals and objectives. Rivalry and competition could take the place of cooperation among schools within the district. In addition, pressure groups may be able to exert greater control over the school. If these pitfalls are to be avoided, so that site budgeting achieves its objectives, decision-makers in the district and at the school site must establish clear policies and effective communication links.

History of the *California School Accounting Manual*

All California school districts are required to monitor and account accurately for all revenues and expenditures. The California Department of Education has responsibility for developing proper forms and procedures for school district accounting.

The first manual for school accounting was developed in 1939 based on information provided by the U.S. Office of Education. This early document contained information on proper accounting procedures for the classification of expenditures as well as definitions of accounting terms. Over the intervening several decades the manual has been revised many times to meet the needs of school districts, the state department, state legislature, governor, school boards, and interested citizens. Added sections have expanded definitions of expenditures, clarified the difference between "supplies" and "equipment," and described accounting procedures to purchase school sites and construct school buildings.

Current procedures are contained in the *California School Accounting Manual*, which the California Department of Education developed with the assistance and cooperation of the California Association of School Business Officials (CASBO). This chapter draws information from that manual. As accounting procedures change and new laws are passed, the manual is revised; revisions are posted on the Website of the California Department of Education.

California's Account Code Structure

The objectives of a standardized school accounting structure are contained in the *California School Accounting Manual*. They are briefly summarized as follows:

- to establish a uniform, comprehensive chart of accounts to improve financial data collection, reporting, transmission, accuracy, and comparability

- to reduce the workload of school employees in preparing financial reports

- to meet federal compliance requirements and to increase opportunities for California districts to receive federal funding

- to ensure that school districts conform to generally accepted accounting principles (GAAP)

- to inform stakeholders of the sources of funds and how they are used.

To accomplish these objectives, the account code structure contains six fields that must be included in the accounting structure of all districts. These fields are:

Fund/Account Group   Resource   Project Year
Goal   Function (Activity)   Object

California districts are permitted to add additional fields in their chart of accounts, but must include the required six. The fields are briefly described:

- **Fund**—Identifies specific activities or defines objectives of the district. Examples include the general fund, adult education fund, and transportation fund. Additional discussion of funds is contained in Chapter 8.

- **Resource**—Records revenues that require special accounting or reporting procedures or that have legal restrictions as to how the funds may be used. Examples include federal programs, lottery funds, and the State Building Fund.

- **Project Year**—Tracks projects that span more than one fiscal year. Typically, this category includes federal grants. An example from the accounting manual includes a bilingual grant from October 1 (the start of the federal fiscal year) 1999 through September 30, 2000, and a second grant from October 1, 2000 through September 30, 2001. Grant activities for state fiscal year 2000–01 would include three months of expenditures for the first grant and nine months of expenditures for the second grant.

- **Goal**—Tracks income and expenditures by the district's instructional goals. Examples include regular classes, classes for gifted students, driver training, and vocational education.

- **Function**—Tracks income and expenditures for services performed to accomplish one or more objectives in the goal field. An example contained in the accounting manual relates to school transportation. To educate students, a district must transport them to school, feed them, and provide health services. Each of these activities is a function.

- **Object**—Tracks expenditures by the service or commodity. Examples include salaries, employee benefits, books and supplies, services, capital outlay, and a section entitled "other outgo."

An example showing how to use account codes is presented in the state accounting manual.

Fund/Group	Resource	Project Year	Goal	Function	Object
01	7155	0	1110	1000	4100

In this example,

Fund 01	is the General Fund
Resource 7155	is Instructional Materials, grades K–8
Project Year	is not required in this example
Goal 1110	is Regular Education, K–12
Function 1000	is Instruction
Object 4100	is Approved Textbooks and Core Curricular Materials

SOURCE: California Department of Education

School District Expenditures

Once revenue has been estimated, all expenses for the coming year must also be estimated. Costs may be divided into those that can be controlled and those that cannot. Costs also may be divided into personnel and non-personnel items. The collective bargaining agreement should be reviewed carefully for costs that may be "hidden," but were nonetheless negotiated and must be included in the budget. Examples of expenses that must be estimated and placed in the budget are described below.

Expenditures decrease net spendable resources. Expenditures include operating expenses; payments toward retirement of long-term debt; and capital outlay for long-term assets such as land, buildings, and equipment. The Education Code limits school district expenditures to the amounts appropriated for the several major expenditure classes by the board of education through the adoption, approval, and revision of the school district budget. The budget and all documents dealing with appropriations must be prepared in accordance with the same classifications as those required to account for expenditures. To facilitate necessary comparisons, financial reports for local use, as well as those prepared for county, state, or federal agencies, follow the same classification plan.

Objects of Expenditure

Objects of expenditure represent all the things, whether goods or services, that may be purchased. The object classification number identifies the type of item purchased or service obtained. All district operational expenses are included in the object codes. Examples include salaries, supplies, and equipment. In the budget document itself, objects of expenditure may be classified in various ways. They may be grouped under summary headings, or they may be presented in great detail. Grouping under summary headings reduces volume, but at the expense of clarity. Greater detail improves understanding, but is costly to produce. In practice, whatever the budget document looks like, the figures are backed up with highly detailed information on income and expenditures. Then, for reporting purposes, this detail is summarized under more general budget classifications.

Districts classify each expenditure by designating the appropriate goal, function, and object codes on requisitions. The principal or department supervisor is responsible for designating the object code when a requisition is completed. However, the district's chief accountant or business manager makes the final decision regarding the classification appropriate to each expenditure. This decision should be made at the time of commitment to the expenditure. The account or accounts to be charged should be selected whenever goods or services are ordered or when certificated or classified employees are employed or reassigned.

Notices of employment, copies of contracts, and other documents relating to expenditures, or to commitments that will become expenditures, should bear the relevant code designations for review and approval by the district governing board and the county superintendent of schools. This information should also be available for the district's auditor. This procedure ensures that questions concerning the classification of expenditures are settled promptly. A decision regarding object classifications may save time in the future if it serves for repeated disbursements, such as monthly salary payments. Such a procedure is vital if the encumbrance plan of accounting is used by the school district. Following are some of the more frequently used object codes.

1000–1900 Certificated Personnel Salaries

Certificated salaries are paid for positions that require a credential or permit issued by the Commission on Teacher Credentialing. All full-time, part-time, and prorated portions of salaries for personnel serving in these job classifications must be charged to the appropriate object code. Salaries paid to an employee on leave of absence are charged in the same manner and to the same account classification applicable when the employee was in active service for the district.

- **1100 Teachers' Salaries**—The 1100 series of object codes is used to record the full-time, part-time, and prorated portions of salaries for all certificated personnel employed to teach the pupils of the district. The salaries for teachers of children in homes or hospitals, all special education resource specialists and teachers, substitute teachers, and instructional television teachers are included in this classification.

- **1200 Certificated Pupil Support Salaries**—This series of object codes is applied to salaries of librarians, social workers, pupil personnel specialists, psychologists and psychometrists, and counselors. Other salaries include those of physicians and other medical professionals.

- **1300 Certificated Supervisors' and Administrators' Salaries**—The salaries of full-time and part-time certificated personnel engaged in instructional supervision are included in this classification. Job titles include superintendent, associate and assistant superintendent, general supervisor, coordinator, director, and consultant, as well as supervisors of special subjects or grades and their certificated assistants. Duties of personnel who are paid from this classification involve activities intended to improve instruction. Examples include personal conferences with teachers on instructional problems, classroom visitations, group conferences with teachers, and demonstration teaching.

- **1900 Other Certificated Salaries**—The 1900 classification is assigned to all certificated personnel who do not fall within one of the categories previously specified. Examples of such personnel are special education or other program specialists, certificated civic center employees, resource teachers not performing duties as a classroom teacher, and certificated noon playground supervisors.

SOURCE: California Department of Education

2000–2999 Classified Personnel Salaries

Classified salaries cover positions that do not require a credential or permit issued by the Commission on Teacher Credentialing. All full-time, part-time, and prorated portions of these salaries are charged to the object codes indicated.

- **2100 Instructional Aides' Salaries**—Salaries paid to instructional aides are charged to this classification. Instructional aides are those employees who perform their duties under the supervision of a classroom teacher or a special education resource specialist teacher.

- **2200 Classified Support Salaries**—This code is used to record the salaries of transportation, food service, maintenance and operations, and instructional media and library employees.

- **2300 Classified Supervisors' and Administrators' Salaries**—Job classifications in this category include supervisory personnel who are business managers, controllers, directors, chief accountants, supervisors, purchasing agents, assistant superintendents, and noncertificated superintendents. Governing board members and personnel commission members, if they receive district compensation, are also charged to this account.

- **2400 Clerical and Office Staff Salaries**—All salaries of clerks, secretaries, accountants, bookkeepers, machine and computer operators, and other personnel in similar positions are charged to this object code.

- **2900 Other Classified Salaries**—All classified salaries not identifiable with object classifications 2100 through 2400 are charged to this object code. Examples include noon supervision personnel, students, community aides, health aides, and building inspectors.

3000–3999 Employee Benefits

The 3000 accounts are used for employers' contributions to retirement plans and health and welfare benefits. This classification is also designated for cash in lieu of benefits for employees, their dependents, retired employees, and board members.

SOURCE: California Department of Education

4000–4999 Books and Supplies

This classification is used for basic textbooks and instructional materials and supplies.

- **4100 Approved Textbooks and Core Curricula Materials**—This account is used for purchase of basic textbooks and supplementary textbooks. Related teacher manuals and teacher editions are also charged to this account. A basic textbook is defined as a volume intended for use by pupils as a principal source of study material for the completion of a subject or course. A supplementary textbook is a volume that covers part or the entirety of a subject or course, but is not intended for use as a basic textbook. Rather, a supplementary textbook is intended to supply information in addition to, or in extension of, information presented in the regular, or basic, text. All approved consumable materials including kits, audiovisual materials, and workbooks are charged to this account.

- **4200 Books and Other Reference Materials**—This classification is used for books and other reference materials used by district personnel. Library books are also included in this category. However, expenditures for books for a new school library or for library expansion are recorded under object classification 6300, Books and Media for New School Libraries or Major Expansion of School Libraries.

- **4300 Materials and Supplies**—Expenditures for all materials and supplies to be used by students, teachers, and other personnel in connection with the instructional program are charged to this classification. Tests, periodicals, magazines, workbooks, instructional media materials, audiovisual materials, and any other supplies used in the classroom or library are included in this category. Supplies for food service, custodial, gardening, maintenance, medical, and office supplies are also charged to this account. However, expenditures for rental of materials are recorded under object classification 5600, Rentals, Leases, Repairs, and Non-capitalized Improvements.

- **4700 Food**—This classification is used to record expenditures for purchase of food used in the food services program. Expenditures for food used in instruction in a regular classroom are recorded under object code 4300, Materials and Supplies.

SOURCE: California Department of Education

5000–5999 Services and Other Operating Expenditures

This classification is used for expenditures for services, rents, leases, maintenance contracts, dues, travel, insurance, utilities, and legal and other operating expenditures. These expenditures may be authorized by contracts, agreements, or purchase orders.

6000–6599 Capital Outlay

All expenditures for the purchase of sites, buildings, and equipment are charged in this group of object codes. Books for a new or materially expanded library may also be charged here. Leases with option to purchase are also included.

- **6100 Sites and Improvement of Sites**—Some of the expenditures in this category include appraisal fees, search and title insurance, surveys, and condemnation proceedings and fees. Costs to remove buildings on newly acquired sites are also charged to this account. Preparation of sites would include grading, landscaping, seeding, and planting shrubs and trees. Also, furnishing and installing—for the first time—fixed playground apparatus, flagpoles, gateways, fences, and underground storage tanks would be identified with 6100 object codes.
- **6200 Buildings and Improvement of Buildings**—The costs of construction or purchase of new buildings as well as additions to and replacements of obsolete buildings are charged to this classification. Other expenses—including advertising, architectural and engineering fees, blueprints, and inspection services—are also recorded in this object code, as are other expenditures for buildings, including plumbing, electrical work, sprinkling, heating, and ventilating.

6300 Books and Media for New School Libraries or Major Expansion of School Libraries

This classification is used to record expenditures for books and materials for new and expanded libraries.

6400 Equipment

This classification is to record initial and additional purchase of items of equipment. The purchase of furniture, vehicles, machinery, and furnishings that are not integral parts of a building or building system would be charged to this classification.

SOURCE: California Department of Education

6500 Equipment Replacement

This category is used to purchase replacement equipment. The criteria for distinguishing equipment from supplies include the following:

- the item will last more than one year
- the item would be repaired, if feasible, rather than replaced
- the item is an independent unit, rather than incorporated into another unit
- the cost of tagging the item for inventory is a small percentage of its cost
- the price exceeds some minimum dollar value established by the district.

SOURCE: California Department of Education

7000–7499 Other Outgo

This object code is used for all other charges and expenses incurred by the district. Charges in this classification include payments for students enrolled in state or county special schools and transfers of funds to charter schools.

SOURCE: California Department of Education

SUMMARY

Program budgeting provides the board of education, staff, and community with specific costs for each program and department. The system uses account codes that identify each program in the district. For example, all charges incurred by the English department at the high school are entered against one specific account so that staff can track the specific costs each year for this particular curriculum area and site.

A careful accounting for expenditures gives a district a much clearer picture of the cost of each program and facilitates planning for the next year's budget. Proper accounting is also of great assistance in end-of-year auditing.

KEY TERMS

Account codes	Incremental (historical) budgeting
Books and supplies	Object codes
California School Accounting Manual	PPBES
Capital outlay	PPBS
Certificated salaries	SBB
Classified salaries	Service and other operating expenditures
Employee benefits	Spendable resources
Fixed costs	ZBB

Discussion/Essay Questions

1. The major reason for program budgeting is to provide information regarding the cost of each individual program. Give an example of one educational program for which program budgeting is utilized. Describe the types of information that could be gleaned from this process.

2. What is the most common type of program budgeting used in school districts? What are the advantages and disadvantages of this type budgeting?

3. Compare and contrast the advantages and disadvantages of PPBS and ZBB.

4. Site-Based Budgeting (SBB) is very popular in California school districts. What are the advantages and possible disadvantages of this budget system?

5. Account codes incorporate six elements: fund/account group, resource, project year, goal, function (activity), and object code. What is the meaning of an object code?

6. Accounting transactions for school district expenditures may be grouped under summary headings or listed in exhaustive detail. What are the major advantages of each approach?

7. Either the principal/program manager or the business manager may have final responsibility for designating the expenditure object code on a requisition. Which of the administrators should have ultimate responsibility and why?

8. Object codes run in a series from 1000s to 8000s. Which group of codes would account for the largest expenditures in a district budget? What expenditures are included in that classification?

9. Textbooks and other books are charged to object codes in the 4000 series. However, books and media for new or expanded libraries are charged to the 6000 series. What is the rationale for this difference?

CHAPTER 8

School District Funds

Money alone sets the entire world in motion.

(Maxim)

Introduction

California school districts use an accounting system known as "fund accounting." This system is also used by other government entities. According to the *California School Accounting Manual* (CDE, 2016), a fund is

an accounting entity with a self-balancing set of accounts recording financial resources and liabilities. It is established to carry on specific activities or to attain certain objectives of an LEA (local educational agency) in accordance with special regulations, restrictions, or limitations. The fund field applies to revenue, expenditure, and balance sheet accounts.

The largest and most active fund is the General Fund. This is the fund within which all the accounts that directly support the educational program are contained. For example, salaries, fringe benefits, textbooks, and instructional supplies are included in the General Fund. Each fund has a separate ending balance that may be divided into restricted and unrestricted accounts. A restricted account may be expended only for certain purposes, while an unrestricted account may be used for any general purpose within the guidelines established for the fund.

Auditors typically audit each fund separately. Therefore, most school districts operate with as few funds as necessary to maintain a cost-efficient system, keeping auditor and staff time to a minimum. The object codes that make up each fund are the same for all funds. For example, the 6400 account (equipment) has the same object code and name in the building fund as it has in the general fund.

Table 5	Selected Types of Funds in California School Districts

General Fund
This is the primary fund for all school district operations. This fund includes both restricted and unrestricted school district revenue and expenditures.

Bond Interest and Redemption Fund (restricted)
These monies are property tax collections used to pay bonded indebtedness.

Building Fund
This fund is for capital improvements. Bond issue receipts and monies from sales of lands are deposited in this account. Building improvements and buses may be purchased from the Building Fund.

Special Reserve Fund
This account may be used for any purpose a board of education designates.

State School Lease-Purchase Fund (restricted)
This fund is used much like the Building Fund.

Cafeteria Special Revenue Fund or **Cafeteria Enterprise Fund** (restricted)
The labor and operational costs for Food Services are included in this fund.

Child Development Fund (restricted)
All funds related to the district Child Development Program are deposited in this fund.

Adult Education Fund (restricted)
This fund is directed to the district's Adult Education Program.

Other
This category may be used for self-insurance reserve.

Deferred Maintenance Fund (restricted)
This account is used for school and district maintenance projects and is partially supported by the state.

Capital Facilities Fund (restricted)
Developers' fees are deposited in and expended from this fund. These are fees collected from builders of new housing to provide schools for the children who will live in the new homes.

Pupil Transportation Equipment Fund (restricted)
Funds from this account purchase school buses and other equipment for transporting students.

Source: California Department of Education

Public School Accounting

Public school accounting requires separate accounting systems for each fund. Accounting for these funds is the basis for the auditors' annual report. In their report, auditors list both income and expenditure accounts and amounts. Table 5 lists the funds utilized by schools in California. Note that some funds are more restricted than others as to how monies may be expended.

Classification and Types of Funds

The Governmental Accounting Standards Board, the National Center for Educational Statistics, and the Association of School Business Officials recommend four major fund classifications, with separate funds in each. The four classifications are:

- Governmental Funds
- Proprietary Funds
- Fiduciary Funds
- Account Groups.

Governmental Funds are divided in turn into the General Fund, Special Revenue Fund, Capital Project Fund, and Debt Service Fund. Proprietary Funds are divided into Enterprise Funds and Internal Service Funds. Fiduciary Funds include the Trust and Agency Fund, and Account Groups contain general fixed assets and general long-term debt.

Governmental Funds

General Fund

The General Fund is the most common type; it is utilized by every school district. All financial resources are accounted for in this fund, which is used to record the ordinary operations of the district. Only those transactions required by law to be handled in another fund are omitted from the General Fund.

Special Revenue Fund

Special Revenue Funds are established to account for the proceeds from specific revenue sources restricted to paying for specified activities or programs. For example, the Adult Education Fund is used to account separately for federal, state, and local revenues for adult education programs. The Cafeteria Fund is used to account separately for federal, state, and local revenue to operate the food service program. Other special revenue funds include the Child Development and Deferred Maintenance Funds.

Capital Projects Funds

Capital Projects Funds are established to account for monies for acquisition or construction of major capital facilities. They are maintained for each capital project in the district. Capital projects usually involve acquiring or building major capital facilities such as land, buildings, or equipment.

Debt Service Funds

Debt Service Funds account for the accumulation of resources for, and the payment of, principal and interest on long-term debt. There are three types of Debt Service Funds: Bond Interest and Redemption Fund, Tax Override Fund, and Debt Service Fund.

School districts typically finance their capital expenditures by selling bonds. A Debt Service Fund is created so that when bond payments are due, funds are available for this expenditure. Proceeds from the sale of bonds are deposited in the county treasury. Any premiums or accrued interest received from the sale of the bonds must be deposited in the Bond Interest and Redemption Fund of the district.

The county auditor maintains control of the district's Bond Interest and Redemption Fund. Principal and interest on the bonds must be paid by the county treasurer from taxes levied by the county auditor-controller.

Proprietary Funds

Proprietary Funds are similar to those used in private industry. Revenue deposited in these accounts comes from such sources as charges for services. Proprietary Funds are divided into two separate parts: Enterprise Funds and the Internal Service Fund.

Enterprise Funds

In some cases, fees are charged for services or merchandise. Examples are funds established by a bookstore, the yearbook, school newspaper, or athletics. Enterprise funds may be used for operations that meet either of two conditions:

- The fund is financed and operated in a manner similar to that employed by private enterprises. The cost of goods or services can be financed and recovered from charges to users.
- The board has determined that revenues earned or expenses incurred are appropriate for capital maintenance, management control, or accountability. For example, the Cafeteria Fund may be recorded as an enterprise fund, rather than a special reserve fund.

Internal Service Fund

Sometimes one department in a school district may perform a service for another department. For example, the printing department typically services several other operations. Similarly, many departments requisition merchandise from the district warehouse. Costs for these internal service centers are documented in Internal Service Funds.

Fiduciary Funds

"Fiduciary" pertains to a trustee or guardian or a person who holds a thing in trust. This fund is used when the district serves as an intermediary in the distribution of funds. The procedure is similar to that of an attorney serving as executor of an estate. To keep track of deposits and expenditures of these monies, a fiduciary fund is established. There are usually two parts to the Fiduciary Fund, one for trust funds and the other for agency funds.

Trust Funds

The district serves as the agent in disbursing monies from Trust Funds. An example is establishment of a fund to continue to pay retirement benefits to employees.

Agency Funds

Examples of Agency Funds include student body monies and the treasuries of teacher and parent organizations. Sources of receipts include fund-raising ventures; student store merchandise; athletic events and student body performances; and income from concessions, publications, and gifts.

Capital Assets

Capital or fixed assets are the largest investment of any school district. Inventory and control of these assets are a major responsibility of a school district. Keeping track of the assets is a major challenge in many districts. Every teacher must remember the yearly requirement to complete an inventory of equipment, maps, and other items that would be classified as a fixed asset. Finding the recorder or map that was loaned to the teacher down the hall is not easy.

There is even the problem of defining a fixed asset. First, "fixed" does not mean unmovable. Districts have adopted policies that define a fixed asset as "one that is tangible; it can be touched, and one that has a useful life of two or more years." For example, the useful life of a computer may be three to five years, while the useful life of a building can be 50 or more years. Education Code Section 35168 requires districts to maintain records of assets that have a market value which exceeds $500.00. Districts are required to keep the following information for each item:

1. Description
2. Name
3. Identification number
4. Cost
5. Date of acquisition
6. Location of use
7. Time and mode of disposal

Keeping track is an important business function that takes time and expertise of the chief business official. A basic requirement is that all school principals should be responsible for all equipment at his or her school. Each school should maintain its inventory and submit that inventory to the district annually for reconciliation with district records.

SUMMARY

To simplify the procedure of collecting and disbursing resources, districts utilize the governmental fund concept. For example, in the Adult Education Fund, income is collected into specific income accounts and disbursed through expenditures accounts—all activity occurring within the fund. A fund is used to meet a specific objective, in this case, support of all adult education activities within the school district.

Most school districts operate with as few funds as necessary to maintain a cost-efficient system. The use of separate funds ensures that revenues and expenditures set aside for specific purposes are not commingled and provides districts with an efficient and accurate accounting procedure. Utilization of this concept also assists the district's auditor in his or her task.

KEY TERMS

Adult Education Fund

Bond Interest and Redemption Fund

Building Fund

Cafeteria Fund

Capital Facilities Fund

Child Development Fund

Debt Service Fund

Deferred Maintenance Fund

Fiduciary Funds

Fixed assets

Fund accounting

General Fund

Government Funds

Government-Wide Statement of Net Assets

Proprietary Funds

Pupil Transportation Fund

Special Reserve Fund

State School Lease Purchase Fund

Discussion/Essay Questions

1. School districts are required to establish a separate fund for several categories of income and expenditures. Describe fund accounting and give the reasons for this accounting procedure.

2. Most California school districts have four different classifications of funds. Name the four types and give a brief description of each classification.

3. The terms "restricted" and "unrestricted" are used to describe the various funds. Explain the meaning of "restricted fund" and give an example.

4. A Debt Service Fund may be used by California school districts. What is the purpose of this type of fund? Give an example of monies that could be collected and spent in this classification.

School Site Budgeting

CHAPTER

9

If you can't stand the heat, get out of the kitchen.

(President Harry S. Truman)

Introduction

President Truman's famous dictum is apropos as school districts move from centralized to school site budgeting. To assume the task of managing resources and expenditures at the site level is a new responsibility for many principals—a responsibility that is welcomed by some and feared by others.

Over the past several years more than a third of the nation's schools have adopted some form of site-based management. This trend is driven by the belief that school districts need to disperse and deregulate the power and authority of the central office (Mitchell & Treiman, 1993). Those who advocate shifting managerial control from central offices to school sites believe that individual schools can make better educational decisions for the students at that site. However, an ERIC Digest (Hadderman, 1999) points out that the principal and other decision-makers at the site need training and performance data. The school must have a clear mission and goals against which financial decisions can be evaluated. Moreover, the principal must use a leadership style that effectively draws others into the decision-making process. Warden (2002) echoes the same advice, citing New York City Public Schools and Edmonton, Canada, as districts where a thoughtful approach to site-based budgeting led to higher student achievement.

The success of the total educational program at any individual school depends on effective leadership in fiscal planning. A principal cannot function as an effective instructional leader unless she is knowledgeable of financial management. As leaders, principals focus on making a school function well for both staff and students. Teachers, support staff, and students must be provided with the necessary equipment, books, and supplies to be effective. The school plant must be maintained as a safe, attractive and comfortable place for students and employees. To accomplish these objectives, the principal must be skilled in planning and developing the budget and in interpreting it to the superintendent, school board, and community.

Site-based budgeting involves decentralization of power in a district and requires that the superintendent and governing board relinquish some of their control over the ways in which funds are spent. This decision is a difficult hurdle in some districts. Allocating a "lump sum" portion of the district budget to a school site is risky and requires a foundation of trust on the part of the superintendent and board as well as a commitment to acquire new skills on the part of site administration and staff.

Developing, monitoring, and accounting for the school site budget is a major responsibility of the principal. In most districts, the school principal is responsible for maintaining and monitoring the budget at the school site. A school budget is a planning document that links educational policy to financial decisions. It contains a school's priorities and serves as a blueprint, or road map, for meeting the objectives of the school. Decisions typically made by the principal and staff include the level of financial support for library and media services, instructional technology, school athletics, music and art programs, and cafeteria services. Hundreds of financial decisions define the priorities of the school and the district.

The degree of site-level responsibility for the school budget varies greatly from district to district. Because of the constraints imposed by district staffing formulas, labor contracts, and provisions of California's Education Code, a principal may have limited discretion as to certificated and classified staffing. In fact, in some districts very few expenditure categories fall under a principal's authority. Even in the most centralized districts, however, a principal usually has some control over the purchase of instructional, office, and custodial supplies, field trips, and conference attendance, with more limited authority over purchase of textbooks and capital outlay equipment.

Other districts, by contrast, may have decentralized many budget decisions to the site level, including management of utility bills, maintenance costs, and capital outlay. In such a district, personnel decisions may also be highly decentralized. For example, a principal may have the authority to increase class size so as to employ a reading resource teacher or an art specialist instead of a classroom teacher. Financial decision-making can be expected to devolve more to the site level as the move toward site-based management gains momentum.

Budget Worksheet

After educational and budget priorities have been established, the school principal develops a preliminary budget worksheet that is used by the district office to establish school accounts for the next school year. The worksheet in Figure 3 is presented as typical of those required by many California districts.

School Site Accounting

The school budget may be handwritten on ledger sheets, entered into a school computer, or managed by direct connection to the district's data processing center. Regardless of the system used, it is important that the principal maintain a very close relationship with the district accounting department to ensure that the school budget is accurate and up-to-date.

2007–2008 PRELIMINARY BUDGET WORKSHEET

1000 ACCOUNTS—CERTIFICATED SALARIES

1110	$ _____	Contract Salaries
1140	$ _____	Substitute Salaries
1150	$ _____	Teacher Salaries—Other Pay (Stipends)
1230	$ _____	Counselor Salaries
1310	$ _____	Administrator/Director/Coordinator Salaries

3000 ACCOUNTS—CERTIFICATED BENEFITS

Benefits must be budgeted. Multiply the totals above by each of the percentages listed for the account. Note that benefit percentages may change.

3331	$_____	Medicare
3501	$_____	Unemployment Insurance
3601	$_____	Workers' Compensation
3101	$_____	State Teachers Retirement System
3411	$_____	Health and Welfare ($567 per month per person)

2000 ACCOUNTS—CLASSIFIED SALARIES

2110	$_____	Instructional Aide Salaries
2210	$_____	Classified Support Salaries
2310	$_____	Classified Supervisors & Administrators
2410	$_____	Clerical & Office Salaries

3000 ACCOUNTS—CLASSIFIED BENEFITS

Benefits for Part-time Employees (Less than 4 hours)

3332	$_____	Medicare
3502	$_____	Unemployment Insurance
3602	$_____	Workers' Compensation

Benefits for Classified Employees (Four hours or more)

3312	$_____	FICA (6.20%)
3332	$_____	Medicare (1.45%)
3412	$_____	Health & Welfare Benefits ($611/month per person)
3502	$_____	Unemployment Insurance (0.65%)
3602	$_____	Workers' Compensation (2.161%)
3802	$_____	Public Employees Retirement System (12.449%)

4000 ACCOUNTS—BOOKS AND SUPPLIES
(Consumable Single Items Costing Less than $500)

4110	$_____	Textbooks
4210	$_____	Other Books
4210	$_____	Other Computerized Books
4310	$_____	Instructional Materials (Vendors/Warehouse, Testing Materials)
4330	$_____	Meeting Refreshments (Snacks, not Meals)
4340	$_____	Computer Software
4350	$_____	Office Supplies
4390	$_____	Other Supplies (Includes Computers)

5000 ACCOUNTS—Services and Operations

5200	$_____	Conference Registration Dues & Memberships Rentals & Leases
5300	$_____	Dues & Memberships
5610	$_____	Rentals & Leases
5630	$_____	Vendor Repair/Maintenance Agreement
5713	$_____	Field Trips
5714	$_____	Print Shop
5715	$_____	Postage
5810	$_____	Contracted Services
5840	$_____	Computer/Tech Related Services (On-Line Services/Site License)
5850	$_____	Professional/Consulting Services
5910	$_____	Communications (Telephone, Ceil Phone, Pager)
5940	$_____	Internet Provider

6000 ACCOUNTS—Capitalized and Inventoried (Single Items Costing $5,000 and up)

6150	$_____	Site Construction (Landscape/Parking Lot/Sidewalks)
6190	$_____	Other Costs—New Site Purchases
6240	$_____	Building Improvement for Technology
6250	$_____	Building Improvement/Construction
6400	$_____	Equipment
6440	$_____	Software Purchases
6450	$_____	Computers & Other Computer Hardware
6500	$_____	Equipment Replacement
6540	$_____	Software Replacement
6550	$_____	Computer-Related Hardware Replacement

Figure 3 Example of a Site Level Worksheet

ROUND TREE ELEMENTARY SCHOOL

Goal	Function	Object	Appropriation	Encumbered	Expended	Balance
1110	1000	1110	$ 500.00	$ .00	$ .00	$500.00
1110	1000	2110	450.00	.00	.00	450.00
1110	1000	4110	1000.00	65.00	.00	935.00
1110	1000	4310	1750.00	438.74	1165.58	145.68
1110	1000	5490	1000.00	800.00	200.00	0.00

Figure 4   Example of a Site Level Budget Spreadsheet

Site budgets usually contain a four-digit object-of-expenditure code, which correlates with the district budget. Expenditure codes may take several forms. Most formats contain a goal code, a function code, and an object code. The budget document also should set out columns for original appropriation, encumbrances, amount expended, and balance. In the sample site budget in Figure 4, the object code 1110 indicates a certificated salary appropriation.

When an order is originally placed, this amount is recorded in the encumbrance column; when the order is received and paid, the amount is placed in the expended column and—if there is a change—an adjustment made to the balance. With inflation and increases in shipping costs, the actual invoice is often more than the cost originally expected. Unless this difference is carefully recorded, the budget may be overspent.

Although most principals delegate the day-to-day responsibilities for maintaining the site budget to a secretary or clerk, a site administrator should check encumbrances and balances frequently to ensure proper accounting. It is particularly important to check the actual cost of books, supplies, and capital outlay against the original invoice.

Using Excel to Build and Monitor the School Site Budget

A school principal may request assistance from the business office for tools to ease the tasks of building and monitoring the budget. Many financial transactions can be monitored more quickly and easily with a personal computer. Some of these tasks include:

- setting up the student body fund
- organizing the site level budget
- maintaining a database of school site personnel.

In several counties, districts are provided with software to project the impact of salary increases and rising costs of fringe benefits, utilities, and other expenditure categories. Such software is also available from commercial firms. With the spread of site-based management, such software may also be useful for administrators at the site level.

This section outlines a task—setting up a school site budget—that can be performed with a software program, Excel, on a Macintosh or PC. The school decision-maker is wise to purchase a handbook for the Excel program and refer to it often. This spreadsheet program is extremely user-friendly and is mastered with little time or trouble. Figure 5 shows a typical school site spreadsheet, including the appropriation, encumbrance, and balance for each account.

	A	B	C	D	E	F	G
1	Goal	Function	Object	Appropriation	Encumbered	Expended	Balance
2	1110	1000	1110	$ 500.00	.00	.00	$500.00
3	1110	1000	2110	$ 450.00	.00	.00	$450.00
4	1110	1000	4110	$1000.00	$65.00	.00	$935.00
5	1110	1000	4310	$1750.00	$438.74	$1165.58	$145.68
6	1110	1000	5940	$1000.00	$800.00	$200.00	.00

Figure 5 Elements of the Spreadsheet

Setting up the Worksheet

Excel conveniently sets up a worksheet, or spreadsheet, with which to develop the budget. A user types the necessary information into each "cell." The worksheet is composed of these cells, each of which is labeled with a letter representing the column (running vertically) and a number representing the row (running horizontally). Thus, the cell in the first column of the first row is cell A1, and so on.

The Help Menu

A user who has difficulty entering data or performing other functions may consult the excellent Help menu within the program. One scans words and phrases that are underlined on the menu, selects one of these phrases, and clicks on it with the mouse. Clicking a term underlined with a solid line jumps to a new position in the help file discussing that term. Clicking a term underlined with a dotted line pops up a small dialog box defining the topic.

Using Excel Functions

Excel offers many shortcuts. The following example shows how to perform a subtraction function. Looking at Figure 5, suppose we want to subtract the numbers in cells E4 and F4 from that in cell D4 to obtain a balance in G4. The formula we would type for cell G4 is as follows:

$$=D4-(E4+F4)$$

This formula gives the balance of $935.00, as indicated in the figure. Such a formula can be copied to other cells in the same column; the formula automatically adjusts itself so that it computes a balance for each row using data in that row.

Functions available in Excel include the following:

Function	Example
Sum	=SUM(W1:W10)
Average	=AVERAGE(X10:X20)
Maximum	=MAX(Y1:Y10)
Minimum	=MIN(Z20:Z45)

The Advantages of Excel

The advantages of Excel are that you can

- create tables of data
- use formulas to calculate new information from data

	A	B
1	Books and supplies	$ 400.00
2	Paper supplies	200.00
3	Equipment	200.00
4	Total	$ 800.00

Figure 6 Site Level Budget

- produce colorful charts based on the data
- save the work so that each month the spreadsheet can simply be updated, rather than re-created.

Organizing the Site Level Budget

To set up a site budget, column A may be used to list expenditure titles and Column B to list dollar amounts, as shown in Figure 6. The budget may be decreased or increased by a percentage amount. The salaries of personnel may be entered in exactly the same way. Column A may be used to list the names of the personnel and column B to list their salaries. Spreadsheet programs such as Excel easily compute simple percentages and may save the financial decision-maker much time.

SUMMARY

Almost all leadership positions in public schools require the management of public funds. Individuals seeking leadership positions in public schools should have a sound foundation in basic budgeting principles and policies. School administrators should understand the accounting system, including the way financial information is recorded, organized, and presented. Since no instructional program can survive without needed resources, the principal who provides strong financial leadership at a school site also has a strong advantage in developing an outstanding instructional program. The business side of the principalship must be mastered if the instructional program is to be successful.

With the current movement toward educational restructuring and decentralized decision-making, far greater control over the budget is placed at school sites. This responsibility calls for additional training for the school administrator and support staff to ensure proper decision-making and accounting for school expenditures.

KEY TERMS

Cells and addresses

Centralized district

Decentralized district

Encumbrance

Fiscal planning

Function code

Goal code

Ledger sheets

Object code

School budget

Spreadsheet

Discussion/Essay Questions

1. The success of the total educational program at any individual school depends on effective leadership in fiscal planning. Do you agree or disagree with this statement? Support your answer with specific examples.

2. Principals are being given greater and greater responsibility for developing a budget at the school site. What are the advantages and disadvantages of this trend?

3. The school budget may be developed primarily at the district ("centralized budgeting") or at each school site ("decentralized"). What are the advantages and disadvantages of centralized budgeting?

4. An accounting procedure referred to as "encumbrance" is widely used by school districts. What does this term mean? Why is it important?

The Annual Audit

Audit independence and sound governance are our best defense against the worst corporate scandals.

(Steve Westley, California State Controller)

Introduction

Today's the day! The auditors will be here at 9:00 A.M. Energy is running high in the business office, and tension is building. Accounting books are stacked in the conference room; tables and desks are cleared; and the coffee is hot. What will they ask for first? This scene could describe any school district office at the onset of the annual audit.

The annual audit, a requirement of the California Education Code, can be viewed in different ways. It may be seen as positive tool—or dreaded with the feeling "They are out to get us." These perspectives vary from district to district and among personnel within a district. For a district employee who takes pride in his or her work, an audit may become a source of accolades—or of anxiety.

Required Audit

Each California superintendent is required by Section 41020 of the Education Code to arrange for an annual audit of all school district funds. This section states, "It is the intent of the Legislature to encourage sound fiscal management practices among school districts for the most efficient and effective use of public funds for the education of children in California by strengthening fiscal accountability at the district, county, and state levels."

Audits must be conducted by an unbiased, independent firm. Only licensed Certified Public Accountants (CPAs) are eligible to perform the audit. Each year, by December 31, the State Controller publishes a list of CPAs qualified to conduct district audits. This independent audit gives credibility to the district report of its financial condition. The annual audit provides assurances that the information shown in the district's financial report is correct, and that no major errors or omissions exist.

The purpose of the annual audit is to provide the governing board and other interested parties with key financial information about the district from an independent perspective. A successful audit adds credibility to the district's financial statements in the eyes of creditors, bankers, investors, and others for whom it is essential to view the financial statements with confidence.

Even if an annual audit were not mandated, good management practices would require it. Each district must contract for its annual audit by April 1. If this task is not completed by the district, the county superintendent must arrange for the audit on the district's behalf. Typically, auditors work with school personnel for many months prior to November, by which time the audit must have been completed.

Each district must have its audit for the previous fiscal year completed and filed with the county superintendent by December 15. If the deadline is not met, the county superintendent may grant an extension, contract with another auditor, or request the state controller to investigate the situation (Education Code sections 41020 and 41020.2).

Fees for the Audit

Fees for the audit are paid by the school district and vary with the size of the district and its geographic location. An audit costs more in smaller districts—those with less than 5,000 ADA—than in districts with higher enrollments. In 2005–06, the statewide ADA average costs ranged from less than $2.00 in districts with 10,000 pupils or more to approximately $26.00 for districts with 1,000 enrollment or less (Westley, 2006).

Audit Guidelines

In 1984–85 the State Controller assumed fiscal oversight responsibilities for California school districts. To implement this responsibility, the controller

- prepares and posts an annual lists of CPAs qualified to conduct district audits
- prepares and updates an audit guide used by CPAs in conducting the annual audit
- reviews CPA audit work-papers to determine if the work performed meets auditing and reporting requirements
- reviews each district's annual report and notifies the district and its auditor as to the report's completeness and compliance with reporting guidelines
- performs follow-up reviews of specific programs and issues as required.

The California Department of Education assists the controller in preparing the audit guide that is used to ensure compliance with each year's audit. The audit guide, which fills a four-inch notebook, is updated continually. As legislation is enacted or new programs authorized by the federal and state governments, the Department of Education reviews the legislation or programs to determine if there are any compliance issues that should be included in the annual audit. These issues are then drawn to the attention of the controller, who has final responsibility for preparing the audit guide. The audit guidelines are disseminated to all certified accounting firms that perform school audits.

Objectives of the Audit

The best sources of information about all fund balances are the annual audited financial statements. In these documents, the audit confirms the fund balances as well as their distribution among restricted and unrestricted funds. The objectives of the annual audit are to determine:

- if the district's financial statements provide a fair and reasonably complete picture of its financial position and activities
- if there is effective control over and a proper accounting for revenues, expenditures, assets, and liabilities
- if reports and claims to state and federal programs contain accurate and reliable data
- if state and federal funds have been spent in accordance with the terms and regulations of these programs.

The annual audit is not designed to uncover every small error, irregularity, or omission, but to find any major or consistent problems.

Audit Procedures

In the early years of auditing, auditors thoroughly examined all district financial transactions. About 1900, as large-scale business enterprises developed, auditors began to use sampling techniques in the auditing process. Since then, not every payroll warrant or purchase order is checked. The purpose of the audit is to ensure that all documents represent fairly the financial condition of the district. The audit provides an independent assessment of the accounting controls of the district.

Nuehring (2002) provides a list of documents that should be available for the auditors. These obviously include all financial records, but other items might be board minutes, organization charts, contracts, the equipment inventory, personnel changes, and grant agreements.

Auditors are responsible for examining the district's bookkeeping and accounting procedures to uncover waste, fraud, and inefficiency. Auditors are also concerned with proper accounting procedures to ensure accuracy and reliability of accounting data. Since the vast share of district funds is allocated to payroll and employee benefits, auditors pay special attention to position control—the allocation, employment, and replacement of personnel in each program. A mechanism should be developed in every district to ensure that personnel allocations are not exceeded without prior approval.

Any factors that might materially affect the financial condition of the district are noted in the audit report. For example, if a lawsuit might affect the district negatively, this is noted as a possible liability.

General Fund

The auditor is required to review the General Fund of the district, as well as individual funds such as student body and cafeteria accounts. The General Fund is the primary focus of the school district audit. The expenditures and income that the district actually received and spent are compared against budgeted amounts. The audit report notes significant differences in the amounts budgeted and actual revenue or expenditures. This information provides a guideline for future budgeting.

The net ending balance is of special interest to the school board, superintendent, and staff. This calculation shows the amount of money that the district has at the end of the fiscal year. It is called the district's savings or reserve. If the ending balance is over or under estimates, the business manager must determine why this situation occurred.

Student Body Fund

Auditors spend much of their time analyzing student body accounts. They examine expenditures to determine whether they were correctly approved by the student body officers and the authorized administrator. High school student body accounts are especially complicated, since food and athletic sales account for much of the activity.

Auditor's Opinion

Upon completion of the annual audit, the district may receive any of three auditor opinions regarding the district's management and accounting practices.

Positive Unqualified Opinion

An unqualified opinion means that no significant deviations from generally accepted accounting principles (GAAP) were noted. Scott (1990), an employee of the auditing firm of Vavrinek, Trine, Day, and Company, sets forth several guidelines for an unqualified opinion:

- The district must have competent employees with experience and education in the specific business area of their assignment.
- The district must have in place an internal orientation and training program designed to familiarize employees with school business.
- A business services handbook should provide detailed policies and procedures.
- Competent auditors should be selected who have the skill, experience, and time commitment to perform the audit in a complete and competent fashion.

Qualified Opinion

A qualified opinion indicates some problem with the financial records of the district. For example, attendance records at the high school may not be kept according to state guidelines. This example may cause the district to experience a loss of funds from the state. Another audit exception might be found in funds of the student body organization in a high school. Unless these are monitored carefully, expenditures or income may not be accounted for correctly.

The most common deviation in California school districts is found in accounting for fixed assets. Because maintaining the inventory requires extensive personnel time and cost, districts often fail to maintain these records according to accepted accounting principles.

No Opinion

If the auditor reports "no opinion," district records are so poor, or even nonexistent, that the auditors cannot form any opinion at all about the financial status of the school district. Consequently, the audit may be delayed until records can be reconstructed—or the auditor may assign a "No Opinion" status.

The sad news for California schools is that 43 districts may face insolvency within the next three years. Two districts received a negative certification in 2016-2017, which means the district cannot meet its financial obligations. Forty-one districts received a qualified certification in that same year. The qualified certification means that the district may not be able to meet its financial obligations. The affected district budgets range from a small district with a budget of less than one-half million dollars to Los Angeles Unified School District with a budget of more than one billion dollars (CDE, 2017).

Noguchi (2017) states that two-thirds of California school districts will have a financial problem within the next three years. Districts may not be able to make payments to employee retirement funds. California Teachers Retirement Fund (STRS) provides for the certificated staff, (teachers, counselors, administrators, etc.). Public Employees Retirement System (PERS) is for the classified employees or support staff such as bus drivers, food service workers, classified management, secretaries and clerks, etc. Noguchi reports that by 2021 the STRS cost will be almost twenty percent of payroll and PERS will exceed twenty-five percent of payroll.

An example of a district that is in trouble is the San Marcos Unified School District located in Southern California. The district paid $5.5 million in certificated pensions in 2012-2013 and that amount will increase to $27.2 million in 2019-2020. The classified pension payment will go from $2 million to $6 million in 2019 (Brennan, 2017). Brennan quotes Randy Walton, San Marcos board member, "Unless there's a dramatic change, you will see school districts literally go under."

The controller (Chiang, 2010) identifies the most common causes of fiscal problems, which result in a qualified or negative certification:

- Deficit spending
- Salary and benefit negotiations
- Declining enrollment
- Special Education and other restricted fund encroachment
- Inadequate reserves

Value of the Audit Report

The audit report is used by the district superintendent, school board, and county superintendent as an independent review of the financial condition of the district. The report may also contain recommendations to improve procedures and increase efficiency in the business functions of the district. The report is useful to state and federal agencies that fund particular programs in the district. Business and commercial agencies also review the report when considering loan extensions or new credit for the district.

Management Recommendations—Theft/Embezzlement

Audits do not always uncover dishonest actions. The audit usually contains management recommendations suggesting ways to improve record keeping and the avoidance of dishonest actions. Recommendations made by the auditor can strengthen and streamline the district's internal controls, as well as its accounting and administrative practices. Implementing these recommendations may help the district reduce operating costs and ensure that existing resources are used in an efficient and economical manner. Ordinarily, the business staff takes steps during the year to address each of the auditor's recommendations so they do not reappear in subsequent audit reports.

Considering the millions of dollars received and managed by school districts, the documented cases of embezzlement and fraud are few in number. This fact is due to the safeguards in place in school district accounting, and the honesty and dedication of school district employees who are responsible for managing school district funds.

When embezzlement or fraud does occur, it receives full coverage by the media and the press. A widely publicized theft occurred in the early 1990s, when the chief business official (CBO) of the Newport Mesa School District was convicted of stealing almost $4 million from the district. The embezzlement of district funds was the largest theft in California school history up to that time. In the embezzlement's wake, the superintendent resigned, a new financial officer was hired, and new financial controls were instituted.

The CBO's lifestyle received widespread news coverage. He owned a mansion in Newport Beach, plus two other homes in California and one in Texas. He also owned a Rolls Royce and two Mercedes Benzes. Parents and teachers expressed anger when, as a result of the theft of the funds, more than 250 district employees lost their jobs (Reyes, 1995, September 12).

In 2001, three California district employees—two superintendents and an accountant—were accused of receiving district funds in violation of the law. In the case of the accountant, who was employed by the Alum Rock School District, the embezzlement was estimated at a million dollars (San Jose Embezzlement, 2001).

A more recent case of embezzlement occurred in 2013. An accountant for the Rialto School District, Judith Oakes, stole approximately $3.1 million from the district's food service program. Mrs. Oakes had worked for the district for 14 years and stole about $4,000 a week from the cafeteria account. The cafeteria funds were collected and processed by Mrs. Oakes prior to depositing the money in the bank. The theft extended beyond the Rialto district as the Rialto District provided food service for 23 other districts. Oakes resigned her position the day after she was charged with the crime. Her bail was placed at $1.8 million, and if found guilty, she could serve 11 years in prison.

The sensational part of the crime revealed that she was caught twice on camera stealing the money and hiding it in her underwear. The two hundred thousand she was stealing annually augmented the $190,000 income she and her husband received each year. As a result of the embezzlement, the superintendent and deputy superintendent were put on administrative leave and eventually lost their jobs with the district (Yarbrough, 2014).

Occasionally, the audit reveals that districts have been underpaid or overpaid. An extreme example occurred in 2007, when State Controller John Chiang (2007, July 5) announced that Los Angeles Unified School District (LAUSD) improperly claimed and was paid $45 million more from the State than it was due for its pupil promotion and retention program. The Controller reported that the state would offset the $45 million from future LAUSD allocations.

Audit Committee

Over the years many school districts have formed a special Audit Committee to enhance fiscal accountability. Audits cost school districts a significant sum of money and staff time. The work of an Audit Committee can reduce these costs and serve as an added safeguard to ensure prudent supervision of a district's finances. An Audit Committee provides a useful service to the district by promoting communication between the auditor on the one hand and the school board and administration on the other. Many districts have found that audit committees improve quality and spread knowledge of financial reporting.

Audit committees should include people who have experience with financial management and the audit process. Its membership should include representatives of the business staff, as well as board members and the chief business officer. It is also prudent to include other community members with expertise in accounting and finance. A local certified public accountant, a banker, or a financial advisor, for example, could introduce an outside, unbiased check on a district's internal controls.

The purposes of the committee should be well defined by board policy or administrative regulation. Some responsibilities of this committee might include reviewing procedures for handling voided checks, security of blank checks, and signature requirements for checks. The committee might also spot-check bills paid and payroll checks issued. Although an internal audit committee is unlikely to identify serious problems, the existence of such a committee tends to make the staff more careful about following procedures and might reduce temptation among some employees to take advantage of the system. It could also reassure school boards and members of the community that public funds are well managed and that proper controls are in place.

An audit committee can be helpful in discussing implementation of management recommendations with the auditors. Effecting all the audit recommendations may be impossible in times of financial constraints. In such situations a multi-year plan might yield necessary controls without further financial distress to the district.

If an extremely complicated issue arises, a district may contract with an auditor to perform an *ad hoc* analysis of the budget. In this situation, the auditing firm may report directly to the board of education. If legal or personnel issues are involved, the report may be presented in closed session.

SUMMARY

Over the last decade, managing financial resources of schools has become an increasingly difficult task. All California school districts are required to complete an annual audit. The audit is an important resource for school boards, administration, and the community. It provides information on the district's financial position, on compliance with various laws and regulations, and on adherence to good management practices. Most important, this information is gathered through independent review by a professional accountant specifically trained to evaluate these areas.

The audit report provides a major source of information about the financial condition of the district and the accounting methods used by the staff. If the audit does not reflect a favorable opinion, board members and the superintendent should be concerned about the fiscal management of the district.

KEY TERMS

Audit

Audit committee

Audit procedures

Audit report

Controller

CPA

District annual report

Management report

Net ending balance

No opinion

Qualified opinion

Student Body Fund

Unqualified opinion

Discussion/Essay Questions

1. It is estimated that superintendents spend a minimum of 30% of their time on budget issues. What are the major budget tasks performed by the superintendent? Why is so much time spent on this responsibility?

2. Discuss the legal requirements for an annual audit of school district budgets and the major functions performed by an auditor.

3. The California State Controller is charged with fiscal oversight of California school districts. What are the major responsibilities of the controller in this area?

4. After completion of a district audit, the auditor may give any of three opinions regarding a district's fiscal condition. Briefly discuss each of the three opinions and their significance for a district.

Student Body Organizations

One of the most valuable resources available to a school principal is the school's student government.

(Arthur Golden, Superintendent, Snowline Unified School District)

Introduction

The student body organization is composed of student leaders elected by their classmates. These leaders offer a valuable source of information and guidance in addressing a wide range of issues that develop within a school community. Student leaders help a principal set the tone for a school and assist in the educational program for all students. Student government participates in such issues as student citizenship, school operations, attendance, student activities, and scheduling and conducting school programs. It helps with serious matters like drugs, alcohol, vandalism, and violence within the school community. School morale and pride flourish in a school that strongly emphasizes co-curricular programs along with the academic schedule.

Student body organizations are an integral part of the educational program in most high schools in California. They expand the opportunities available in the regular school setting and provide valuable training for students. Among student organizations are athletic teams, music groups, academic groups, and social groups. Depending upon the size of the school, these groups may number several hundred. A guiding principle for all student body organizations should be maximum student involvement.

Management of and accounting for student body funds are major tasks in many schools, their complexity depending on the size of the school and the extent of its activities. In most schools, the principal has primary responsibility for supervision of student body organizations. In a large high school, he or she may delegate this task to a student activities director, although ultimate responsibility for supervising the program still rests with the principal.

In many schools, particularly secondary schools, the sheer number of student body accounts is a nightmare for the student body clerk and for the principal, who retains ultimate accountability for them. As for school site budgets, discussed in previous chapters, computer software programs promise to ease the accounting burden. A major source of information for proper accounting of student body funds is a document, available from the California Department of Education, entitled *Accounting Procedures for Student Organizations* (CDE, 1992). This book is an invaluable tool for accounting personnel and the principal. Guided by this document, districts adopt guidelines for Student Body Fund accounting. If the guidelines are followed and legal entries made on an ongoing basis, the time spent on this task is minimized.

California's Fiscal Crisis Management Assistance Team (FCMAT) developed a new manual in 2015 to assist in the management of ASB accounts: *ASB Accounting Manual, Fraud Prevention*. The book is specifically designed for principals, ASB directors, and classified employees who manage the student store and other student activities.

The Tracy Unified School District has developed an ASB Accounting Guide for use in that district. It is an excellent document and a supplement to the State Accounting Guide: *Accounting Procedures for Student Organizations*. It can be located at the Tracy District website.

Legal Status and Purpose of Student Body Organizations

Education Code Section 48930 and the sections following provide the legal framework for the Student Body Fund. Since student organizations are not supported by public funds, they rely on fund-raising to finance their activities. In raising and expending student funds, the student body organization has one basic aim: to promote the general welfare and morale of the students as a whole. Student body funds exist for the sole purpose of supporting non-instructional activities that enhance the overall educational experience of students.

The school district governing board serves as the legal authority for establishment of the fund. The board must adopt regulations that govern student body organizations, supervision of their activities, and financial operations and management. Governing boards must establish procedures for preparation and control of the student body budget. Student body organizations may be allowed to use school properties without charge, subject to regulations set by the school board. These regulations usually delegate day-to-day management of the student body to the school principal.

Establishment of Student Body Organizations

When a governing board authorizes establishment of a student body organization, several steps should be taken. A constitution must be written that states the name and purpose of the organization. Minutes should be kept of each meeting and a procedure developed to authorize expenditures. Policies should be developed for approving the student body budget, for fund-raising activities, and for election of officers.

The student body usually acts as an umbrella for several clubs and organizations at a school. Specific procedures should be developed for recognition of school clubs and organizations. A primary requirement is that the group be composed entirely of students enrolled at the school. Student groups must receive approval from the student body organization and the school board or its designee. Often, school boards delegate this responsibility to the school principal.

Each student body organization must develop a realistic budget. The principal or student body advisor trains, guides, and supervises students in this task. A preliminary budget is submitted to the student governing body by May 1 each year. Ordinarily, the budget is reviewed and finalized in October. A budget should include estimated income and expenditures. A reserve should be projected to allow a degree of flexibility in case of unanticipated needs.

Student Activities

A majority of funds generated by student body organizations come from fund-raising activities. These activities must promote the general welfare and morale of the entire student body. Some fund-raisers are held at school; others may be outside. Examples of fund-raisers include candy and magazine sales, car washes, dinners, carnivals, and newspaper drives.

Strict federal and state regulations govern sale of food items on campus. Such sales must be authorized by the school board. No food items prepared on the premises by students may be sold during the school day. In elementary schools, food items may be sold after the close of the midday food service period. In high schools, junior highs, and middle schools, food items may be sold at any time during the school day, as long as they are not prepared on the premises and the item is not sold by the district food services program on that school day.

Each plan for fund-raising by a student body organization must be approved by the student council and the school principal. The plan must include a recommended method of financial accountability. Fund-raising efforts must be scheduled carefully to avoid conflict with other departments or organizations and should be limited to minimum interference with the school's educational program.

Student Body Activity Cards

Activity cards are commonly sold to high school students. Funds generated by the sale of student body cards can be substantial. In most high schools, the card is priced from $15 to $50. In a school of 2,000 if half of the student body purchases a card, the revenue ranges from $15,000 to $50,000.

These cards typically provide a variety of benefits, including admission to athletic events and school dances, a discount on the yearbook, and copies of the school newspaper. Members of the student council should give careful thought to items furnished to purchasers of a student body card. For example, should the yearbook be included—or purchased separately? The student body organization should set the price of both the student body card and admission to athletic and other school activities. The benefits associated with a student body card should be printed on the card so students know exactly what they are.

Athletics

Fund-raising connected with athletic events must accord with league agreements and conform to policies of the California Interscholastic Federation (CIF). Income may be generated by sale of pre-numbered tickets, the receipt of a guaranteed amount from schools visited, and exercise of radio and television rights. In many schools with a strong athletic tradition, program sales and concessions at the games also generate substantial income.

Other Fund-Raising Activities

A variety of other sources may yield profit for student organizations. Publications, vending machines, a student store, school dances, musical events, and donations are utilized by most

Table 6	Fundraising Activities *Not* to Be Used

Activity	Reason Inappropriate
Raffles	Element of gambling
Games of chance	Element of gambling
Animal rides	Safety
Activities involving darts or arrows	Safety
Throwing objects at live targets	Safety
Dunking a person into a water tank	Safety
Destroying old cars or similar objects with hammers, etc.	Safety
Selling used jewelry	Health factors
Rummage sales	Health factors
Trampolines or mini-trampolines	Safety

Source: CASBO, 1988.

student body organizations. On the other hand, the California Association of School Business Officials (1988) suggests several activities that should *not* be used to raise funds. These items are listed in Table 6.

Student Fees

The big day has finally arrived. Mom and Dad are so proud of son John, who just graduated from the eighth grade—and with honors, too. The middle school experience is finally over, and John's parents are looking forward to being the parents of a high school student: enrolled in honors math and English, Spanish and biology, band, and athletics. They have never had to worry about John's grades and are very proud that he will be in the band and on the freshman football team. Yes, high school should be smooth sailing.

But what is this during freshman orientation? A $100 calculator for math; $125 to rent his saxophone; $75 for gloves, shoes, and socks for band, plus a $20 fee to sign up; a $30 lab fee in biology; $35 for a field trip to the Museum of Tolerance as part of honors English class; and more than $200 for shoes and athletic equipment to play on the freshman football team. The coach said John would need to bring money for meals before and after football games, too.

The shock that John's parents experienced is not unusual in the public schools of California. Yet these fees are strictly illegal, according to Donald Driftmier (1997), an accountant with Vavrinek, Trine, Day & Company, one of the state's largest auditing firms for California schools. The fees and fund-raisers that keep many programs afloat in public schools conflict with the free education promised in the California Constitution. Driftmier maintains that schools cannot legally charge students to join clubs, band, or athletic programs—or to buy pencils, paper, workbooks, novels, computer disks, calculators, or uniforms. Students may be charged for lunch, or a fee to purchase material for a project the student will take home, such as materials for a wood shop project. However, if the student does not want to take the project home, he need not pay. Students may also be charged for damage or loss of a book or other school property.

Students can voluntarily participate in fund-raisers, but they cannot be excluded from any activity because they do not or will not help raise money. Driftmier said that the law is not followed for two reasons: one is lack of knowledge on the part of teachers and school administrators, and the other is unwillingness to abide by the law. Driftmier advises the districts he audits that they can meet the legal requirements without losing their programs. Schools need to make sure that they clearly tell parents that the fees or charges are voluntary and explain that they are necessary for the programs to continue. Mentioning that financial assistance is available is not good enough.

In 2000 three parents sued the Pasadena school district demanding a halt to the collection of student activity fees and asked for a refund of money already paid for ID cards, athletic clothes, and notebook organizers. The lawsuit, filed in Los Angeles Superior Court, charged that the practice of collecting fees for extracurricular activities is unconstitutional. The plaintiffs argued that such fees violate the free education clause of the California Constitution and that a 1984 state Supreme Court decision had outlawed charges for extracurricular activities. This decision, *Hartzell v. Connell,* had established that extracurricular activities such as band and cheerleading are part of the education program and must be provided without fees (Winton, 2000).

The Los Angeles Superior Court followed *Hartzell,* defining 15 items for which students could not be charged and requiring the district to refund such fees for the preceding three years. Some items, such as field trip costs and the price of lost textbooks, were identified as acceptable charges. Although a superior court decision is not binding across the state, the parents' attorney and a district official expressed their views that the decision would nevertheless affect practices of districts statewide (Winton, 2001).

In 2010, the American Civil Liberties Union (ACLU) informed the San Diego Unified School District that fees were being charged at some San Diego schools. Fees that were cited included $1000 for cheerleading, $545 for the band membership, and $300 to pay for instruments, uniforms, festival entry fees, and coaching (Hoag, 2010).

A settlement was reached that year stating that when the district's auditor finds that illegal fees have been charged, the district must reimburse parents or suffer a financial penalty. California's state Controller, John Chiang, said, "Our public schools aren't free if students are being nickel-and-dimed for the tools required to learn." He continued, "My office is committed to proving the auditing direction necessary" (Blume, 2010).

The State Controller's threat did not stop schools from charging fees. In an attempt to deal with the problem, Governor Brown signed AB 1575 in 2013, which was intended to once and for all stop schools from charging fees. The law stated that all California schools may not charge fees for a student to participate in any educational activity (CDE, 2013). Will a student never again be charged a fee to go to cheerleading camp or the purchase of shoes to be on the football team? As districts face budget cuts the temptation is still there.

Managing Income of a Student Body Organization

As just indicated, a primary activity of student body organizations is fund-raising. Before monies from the Student Body Fund may be spent, several safeguards must be in place. In particular, all expenditures must receive prior approval, either as part of the approved student body budget or by action recorded in the minutes of a meeting. Moreover, the Student Body Fund should be used to benefit those students who are currently active members of student organizations and have assisted in generating such funds; therefore, large Student Body Fund reserves are discouraged (California Association of School Business Officials, 1988). Gorton (1983) identified several additional items to be given attention in managing student body organizations:

- school board authorization for the collection of student activity fees
- involvement of students and teachers in establishing and setting the amount of student activity fees and in decisions about how monies are to be spent

- maintenance of school records of monies collected and disbursed, showing that the procedures enumerated below are being followed:

  A receipt is issued to each individual from whom money is received.

  A deposit receipt is obtained from the bank to show that all monies have been deposited upon receipt.

  The amount that is deposited is recorded in a student activities account under the appropriate fund.

  A requisition form, requiring the signature of the activity sponsor, is used to initiate purchases. Purchases involving large sums of money require the approval of the principal.

  School checks are used to expend monies and to pay student activities bills.

  All expenditures are recorded in the student activities ledger, where each is listed under an appropriate fund.

- monthly preparation of a budget status report for each activity sponsor and for the school administrator

- yearly audit and review of the purposes for which student activity monies have been spent, conducted by the district office with involvement of the school principal and sponsors of activities.

In addition to these guidelines for managing and tracking student organization funds, state regulations prohibit certain expenditures, including:

- equipment, supplies, forms, and postage for curricular or classroom use or for district business

- repair and maintenance of district-owned equipment

- salaries or supplies that are the responsibility of the district

- articles for the personal use of district employees

- gifts, loans, credit, or purchase of accommodations for district employees or other personnel

- contributions to fund-raising drives for charitable organizations (CDE, 1992).

Because of the volume of student body activities, all monies must be subject to careful collection and verification procedures. Any money collected from any source must be substantiated by pre-numbered student body receipts, pre-numbered auxiliary receipts, pre-numbered class receipt records, cash registers supplying cumulative readings, or other auditable records.

All fund-raising activities must be approved by the principal and the student body organization. Pre-numbered tickets should not be printed in the school printing department. All forms should be controlled by the principal or his or her designee. Whenever tickets are sold, ticket reports and unsold tickets must be available for audit. Whenever possible, money must be collected in the central office. Collections should be deposited in the bank daily—and never left in the school over weekends or holidays.

Accounting procedures for student store sales, sales of food items, fees collected for athletic events, concessions, publications, gifts and grants, yearbook sales, and proceeds from vending machines should be carefully established and monitored. Procedures for the purchase and lease of equipment also should be developed. A number of state and federal regulations, several of which have been noted above, control the sale of food by members of the student body.

Chart of Accounts and Financial Reports

A chart of accounts should be developed by the student body organization to track revenue and disbursements in the various student body groups. Account numbers should correspond to district and state accounting procedures. Accounts include current assets, fixed assets, current liabilities, trust

**ALVORD UNIFIED SCHOOL DISTRICT
LA SIERRA HIGH SCHOOL
STUDENT BODY BUDGET 2010–2011**

Account	Activity	Balance 6/30	Income	Expenditures	Balance
200.11	Class of 2011	9,634	500	9,520	614
200.12	Class of 2012	(3184)	71,000	60,500	7,336
200.13	Class of 2013	111	600	3,700	(2,989)
200.14	Class of 2014	300	700	450	550
205.00	ANIME CLUB	53	75	80	48
206.00	Academic Decathn	245	775	800	220
207.00	ART CLUB	2710	880	2,300	1290
208.00	AVID	278	8,600	8,750	128
210.00	Baseball	15	0	74	0
211.00	All American Club	74	0	74	0
212.00	Band/Color Guard	184	1,200	1,150	214
213.00	Black Student Union	772	550	875	447
214.00	Boys Basketball	0	4,875	4,850	25
215.00	Boys Tennis	621	880	1,050	451
216.00	CSF	1,760	200	1,150	810
217.00	College Club	800		775	96
218.00	Cross County	3,025		5,100	996
220	Drama	11,500		14,600	1,125.00
221.00	Debate Club	0		0	0
224.00	Chess Club	345		350	116
226.00	Lang Club	0		0	0
231.00	Football	850		1,925	324

Figure 7   Sample Student Body Budget

accounts, other liabilities, other accounts, revenues, and expenditures. Trust accounts are generally divided into three main groups: scholarship accounts, class accounts, and club accounts.

Student body officers develop periodic financial reports. A report, or financial statement, lists revenues and expenditures and concludes with a balance sheet. This information compares actual revenue and expenditures with budget projections. In a large high school, financial statements should be prepared on a monthly basis; in a smaller school, with fewer organizations and accounts, a bimonthly statement may be sufficient. Whatever the timeline, these reports enable students, advisors, the principal, and the school board to monitor the financial condition of the organization and to make adjustments where required. Figure 7 provides an example of a Student Body Financial Report.

Auditing of Student Body Accounts

A major responsibility of the principal is to ensure that student body accounts are properly maintained. All books, transactions, and records of the Student Body Fund must be open to review and audit. The district is required to perform periodic internal audits and to conduct an annual external audit. Like the audit of all other district funds and accounts, the audit of the Student Body Fund must be performed by an accountant licensed by the State Board of Accountancy who is not otherwise employed by the district.

The California Association of School Business Officials developed the following six guidelines to assist school officials in complying with proper accounting procedures:

- Checks should never be issued to cash

- A complete reconciliation should be kept of cash collected and disbursed; any remaining funds are to be deposited
- Site checkbooks used for field trips should be controlled by the site secretary or a student body controller
- No blank checks should be issued to pay for field trips
- Outside organizations (e.g., booster club, P.T.A.) who sponsor field trips should carry their own insurance, proof of which should be filed at the district office
- All outside organizations are responsible for collecting and depositing funds related to any of their sponsored events
- School personnel are not to sign checks or invoices, do bookkeeping, or serve as an officer of an outside organization (Driftmier, 1997).

The California Education Code requires that district funds pay the cost of the audit. This requirement is intended to ensure strict objectivity by the auditor. The busy principal may find the laws, rules, and regulations related to the Student Body Fund complex and time-consuming. The results are worth the effort, however, because a well-managed program of student organizations pays rich dividends to the principal and staff and safeguards the integrity of the organizations themselves.

SUMMARY

Student body organizations have a very important role in the functioning of a school. They represent an important addition to the educational experiences of students. Regardless of the size of these organizations or the dollar volume of fund-raising activities, the level of accountability must match that required of other funds within the district.

A school district governing board, the superintendent, business manager, and principal have major roles to perform in effective management of a student body organization. Carefully crafted policies, regulations, and guidelines need to be developed to ensure proper accounting for student body funds. A major source to guide the financial aspects of a student body organization is contained in a California Department of Education publication entitled *Accounting Procedures for Student Organizations* (1992).

It is important to recognize that a major objective of the student body organization is instructional in nature. The decision-making experience involved in developing and managing the student body organization can be invaluable. Students should be provided as much latitude in decision-making as is reasonable, with proper guidance from the principal and staff.

KEY TERMS

*2015 ASB Accounting Manual,
    Fraud Prevention Guide*

*Accounting Procedures
    for Student Organizations*

ASB

ASB Constitution

Assembly Bill 1575

Charitable organizations

Chart of accounts

CIF

Fund-raising activities

Pre-numbered tickets

Student activities

Student body cards

Student body fund

Student body reserves

Trust accounts

Discussion/Essay Questions

1. Effective leadership in the Associated Student Body (ASB) can be a great asset to a school's instructional program. Discuss the instructional benefits of the ASB.

2. Discuss the major responsibilities of the principal in supervising the ASB.

3. Student body activity cards may account for a considerable sum of revenues and expenditures in a school. What are the major purposes of the student body card? What accounting safeguards should be established for managing this program?

4. Gorton (1983) discussed several key items in managing student body organizations. What are these key elements?

Transportation

CHAPTER

12

Students are nearly eight times safer riding in a school bus than in cars.

(U.S. Department of Transportation, National Highway Traffic Safety Administration)

Introduction

Every kindergarten parent worries about the safety of his or her children as they climb aboard the school bus for that first day of school. Is that big yellow bus safe, or should I drive my child to school?

The National Highway Traffic Safety Administration (NHTSA) is responsible for the vehicle safety standards of the nation's school buses. This agency reports that school buses transport 26 million of the 50 million students to school each day. The nation's cost of student transportation is approximately $22 billion each year with 55 percent of K-12 students riding the bus each day (NHTSA, 2017).

This agency reports that the school bus is the safest vehicle on the road. A child is much safer taking a bus to and from school than traveling by car. Students are 70 times more likely to get to school safely when taking a school bus instead of traveling by car (NHTSA, 2017).

A major reason for the safety of the school bus is that school buses are the most regulated vehicles on the road. They are designed to be safer than passenger vehicles in preventing crashes and injuries. For example, every state requires all school buses to have the warning lights when the bus is loading and unloading students (NHTSA, 2017).

The History of School Bus Transportation

What was once a rural phenomenon has become an accepted, even expected, service in most California communities. Transportation of students to and from school began when the country entered the automotive age. Busing helped make education available to a greater number of children. The busing of students also contributed to the reduction or elimination of the one-room school, as rural students were transported to nearby villages or cities.

In an earlier era it was not uncommon that a teacher, the principal, or some other staff member drove the school bus in addition to his or her primary job. With modern improvements in transportation vehicles and construction of modern roads and freeways, the task of driving a bus has become far more complex and in California, as in most states, is strongly regulated by the state department of education and the highway patrol.

Today, many students ride school buses, rather than public transportation, to reach school. Special education students often need transportation, even for short distances, and often on vehicles designed to carry equipment such as wheelchairs. In addition to conveying students to and from school, many district transportation systems also carry students to and from a vast array of co-curricular activities, including athletic events and field trips. With increased enrollments and shifting populations come overcrowded classrooms, again leading to transportation to move young people from one school to another. School business officials agree that managing transportation has become a demanding, often frustrating, task and a drain on fiscal resources.

School transportation has come a long way since the horse-drawn wagon. Steve Hirano (2000) developed a summary of the key events that shaped the development of school transportation. With permission of the author, a brief summary of those events follows.

- **1900—Turn of the century.** Eighteen states had laws that approved public funding for pupil transportation.
- **1920—The first school bus chassis.** A 20-seat passenger bus was developed by International Motor Car Company.
- **1926—North Carolina contract for 200 school buses.** Perley A. Thomas Car Works, a streetcar manufacturer, won a contract to manufacture 200 school buses for the state.
- **1939—The first national school transportation conference.** Representatives from the 48 states attended the seven-day conference. The delegates created 44 standards for buses. Among those standards was use of the color yellow.
- **1954—*Brown v. Board of Education.*** This U.S. Supreme Court decision called for elimination of segregated schools. Its effect on school transportation was to create crosstown busing in many cities.
- **1956—Stopping for school buses.** New York was the first state to approve a law requiring motorists to halt for stopped school buses.
- **1959—First diesel school bus.** The first diesel school bus in the United States was put into operation in North Carolina. Today, it is estimated that 95% of all school buses are diesel-powered.
- **1975—Education of all Handicapped Children Act.** This federal legislation guaranteed a "free and appropriate public education for all children." The legislation greatly expanded the role and cost of school bus operations.
- **1977—Federal Safety Standards.** New federal standards for school bus construction went into effect. The standards dealt with emergency exits, roof strength, seating, fuel system integrity, and hydraulic brake systems.

- **1986—Safety Belts.** New York became the first state to mandate seat belts in all new school buses. The legislation did not mandate use of the belts.
- **1995—Drug and Alcohol Testing.** All districts with 50 or more drivers were required to implement an alcohol and drug testing program for drivers. In 1996, new legislation was approved that required all districts, regardless of size, to implement the testing program.

Policy Issues

In many California districts the chief business official supervises the transportation department. As districts become larger, this responsibility may be delegated to a lead bus driver or a transportation supervisor. As the business manager develops a plan for student transportation, consideration should be given to the following policy questions:

- Is the transportation system to be used solely to transport students to and from school?
- If it is used for the athletic and co-curricular programs, are there guidelines for mileage, overnight stays, etc.?
- What are state and district walking distances for children of various ages and grades?
- What training programs are in place for bus drivers, mechanics, dispatchers, and supervisors?
- Is it financially and politically wise to contract for student transportation?
- Are routing and scheduling managed in an economical fashion?
- Have long-range plans been made for bus replacement—a major capital outlay expenditure?
- Are accounting methods in place and adequate for proper filing of claims for state reimbursement?

Financing School Transportation

The American School Bus Council (AMSBC, 2013) estimates that approximately 26 million (53%) U.S. students ride the school bus each school day. In California, a smaller percent, 12%, students ride the bus each day (LAO, 2014).

While many California School Districts are eliminating student transportation, the Los Angeles School District continues to operate the third largest fleet in the nation. The district has a fleet of 1,700 buses and transports nearly 45,000 students each day (Schlosser, 2017, December, 5).

The number of California students who ride the bus has declined from 25% to 12.5% over the last couple of decades. There are a number of reasons why ridership has dropped. The loss of state funding has been a major factor, and with less funding several districts have eliminated or partially reduced home-to-school transportation by increasing walking distance or eliminating some routes (LAO, 2014).

While several California school districts are eliminating home to school transportation, other districts are finding ways to reduce cost. Districts are reducing fuel cost by moving to electric buses or natural gas. In 2017 sixteen southern California school districts were awarded new electric school buses by the South Coast Air Quality Management District. Other districts are purchasing buses powered by natural gas (Tuvalu, 2017).

Computerized School Bus Routing

Computerized school bus routing has enabled many districts to reduce transportation costs. Several software programs have been written for this purpose. An Internet search turned up several companies offering such programs for school districts. This technology can develop optimum schedules for picking up students and delivering them to drop-off points near their homes, calculate walking distances from bus stops to student homes, find more economical and timesaving routes, provide special schedules for handicapped students, lay out field trips, and schedule employees.

Auditing Bus Routes

After all bus routes are established and stabilized for the year, the system must be audited. One way to accomplish this task is to place timers on buses to record the time necessary for pre-trip inspection, cleaning, and actually driving the route. Motion timers are easily installed. The timer records the time the driver starts the route and continues recording until the route is completed. The timer also records any unauthorized stops that occur along the way.

The transportation director should monitor all routes for at least two days and record the mileage each day. Time requirements are calculated and additional time added for such duties as warm-up and cleanup. The data collected through this system are useful for payroll and for auditing purposes.

Preventive Maintenance

The key to a safe, efficient transportation system is well-maintained equipment. Preventive maintenance pays off financially. For example, properly inflated tires increase fuel efficiency, safety, and the life of the tire. Inspection and maintenance are scheduled and tracked for each vehicle. Two additional transportation issues of importance are bus replacement and district charges for home-to-school transportation.

Student Safety and Seat Belts

Since safety belts were first installed on automobiles, the question has been, "Would seat belts on school buses provide for greater safety?" Several studies have been conducted to answer this question. A major study was completed by the National Highway Traffic Safety Administration (NHTSA) in 2000. The study concluded that there was no supportable need for lap belts in large school buses.

However, the California Legislature, in 1993, approved Assembly Bill 15, which required that all school buses manufactured on or after January 1, 2002, would have safety belts. The legislation required pelvic and upper torso restraints. Implementation was delayed when Senate Bill 568 was approved. This legislation requires seat belts in Type II buses (carrying no more than 16 passengers) manufactured after July 1, 2004, and in Type I buses (designed for carrying more than 16 passengers) manufactured after July 1, 2005. This requirement has significant implications for districts as they consider:

- The seat belts will reduce school bus capacity from 17 to 33%, depending on the bus and its floor plan.

- Who will be responsible for ensuring that students are wearing the seat belts?
- What are the liability and insurance implications?

One hopes that these questions will be answered in due time (Wigginton & Hunter, 2004).

States Test-Drive Hybrid School Buses

Eight states are test-driving a new hybrid school bus. Napa Valley School District is the first in California to purchase the hybrid bus. The hybrid bus operates on a similar principle to the hybrid car, a combination of diesel and electricity. The bus gets about 12 miles per gallon as opposed to the 7 or 8 miles achieved by a conventional bus. The catch is the bus costs in excess of $200,000, about double the price of a conventional bus. However, if the number of orders increases for the buses, the cost will decrease (Hoffman, 2007).

In 2014, Kings Canyon School District made the news with the purchase of four all-electric buses. The district estimates a saving over $10,000 a year in fuel and maintenance costs. The electric bus has a range of 80–100 miles and holds 25 students or 18 students with a wheelchair. The buses are partially funded by the state's air quality program (Dechert, 2014).

Transportation Fees

In an attempt to offset transportation costs, several California districts began charging student transportation fees. In 1988 the U.S. Second District Court found such fees unconstitutional. However, in April 1991, California's Third District Court of Appeals ruled just the opposite, declaring that home-to-school transportation fees are legal. Since the two cases were in conflict, the California Supreme Court agreed to hear an appeal of the Third Court's decision. In 1992 the California Supreme Court ruled in *Arcadia Unified School District v. State Department of Education* that it is legal for school districts to charge a fee for home-to-school transportation as long as students who cannot afford to pay are exempted from the fee.

The two key issues reviewed in the Arcadia case were these:

- Does the law allowing school districts to charge fees for home-to-school transportation (Education Code 39807.5) violate the free school guarantee in the California Constitution?
- Does the law allowing school districts to charge fees for home-to-school transportation violate the equal protection clause of the California Constitution?

Six of the seven Supreme Court Justices concluded that the answer to both questions was "no." The court's rationale for this decision was that students are not required to use the same means of transportation as their classmates in order to get to school. Individual students may choose different modes of transportation to suit their own circumstances. Unlike textbooks or teachers' salaries, transportation is not an expense peculiar to education. Without doubt, school-provided transportation may enhance or be useful to school activity, but it is not a necessary element that each student must utilize or be denied the opportunity to receive an education, according to the court.

When establishing a fee policy, a district must develop an exemption for parents and guardians who are indigent. Districts may define "indigent" in either of two ways. The same criteria established for the free lunch program may be used, or students whose families are recipients of CalWORKS, formerly Aid to Families with Dependent Children (AFDC), may be exempt from transportation fees. In addition, handicapped students eligible for transportation fee exemptions are those whose Individualized Education Plans (IEPs) specify transportation services.

When developing a fee policy, a district must consider two additional requirements of the Education Code. The fees collected in any year may not exceed the statewide average unsubsidized cost of providing transportation on a public transportation system. Neither may they be higher than the district's actual operating cost of home-to-school transportation minus state aid for transportation. In addition, the school board must avoid provisions that carry implications of racial or ethnic segregation.

Fees for Extracurricular Activities

The California Supreme Court decision in *Arcadia* also addressed fees for extracurricular activities. In upholding a fee for home-to-school transportation, the California Supreme Court differentiated a transportation fee from a fee for extracurricular activities. In 1984 the Supreme Court had ruled in *Hartzell v. Connell* that a fee for extracurricular activities violates the free school guarantee embedded in the California Constitution. The court held that the free school guarantee extends to all activities that constitute an integral and fundamental part of elementary and secondary education or that constitute necessary elements of any school's activity. Therefore, the decision in *Arcadia* does not authorize fees for transportation connected to extracurricular activities (Atkinson, Andelson, Loya, Ruud, & Romo, 1992).

Contracting for Service

With a view to conserving district funds, several California school districts contract with outside firms for student transportation services. The major advantage of contract services for many districts is avoiding capital expenditures for buses. With one bus costing approximately $100,000, vehicle purchases are a major drain on the resources of most districts. Moreover, some districts conclude that contracting for service reduces the annual operational cost of transporting students.

When considering contracting for services, the district should examine the most important variable in student transportation services: transporting students safely and efficiently. Selection of a contractor should start with a thorough understanding of the student transportation needs of the district. That in place, the district is ready to select a contractor who can provide a competitive bid that meets all district requirements, chief among them a safe and effective system.

The goal in writing the transportation contract is to develop a strong working relationship between the contractor and the district. To that end, the contract should be precisely written and reviewed by the district's attorney. Elements to be covered in the contract include management of services, pupil delivery times, training requirements for drivers, safety standards, and vehicle maintenance standards. Procedures for evaluating the services of the contractor are essential. Included in the contract must be a termination clause to be invoked if services are not provided as agreed upon.

SUMMARY

Student transportation is big business in California. With many rural communities that cover hundreds of square miles, student transportation has become a major cost factor in many districts. Overcrowding of schools in urban areas has also resulted in higher transportation costs as young people are moved from one site to another. School boards and superintendents have attempted to offset the skyrocketing costs of student transportation with various strategies, including longer student walking distances, staggered starting and ending times for schools, and fees for student transportation.

Providing safe and efficient student transportation is a formidable problem facing the legislature and taxpayers of this state. Every day, thousands of students are transported to and from school in buses that were manufactured before the federal safety standards developed in 1977. Of California school buses, 9% were constructed prior to 1977, the highest percentage in the nation. Only two other states, Washington (8.68%) and Louisiana (6.9%), utilize more than 5% pre-1977 buses ("Pre-1977," 2000). A major capital investment is required to replace these buses.

KEY TERMS

Arcadia Unified School District v. State Department of Education

Auditing bus routes

Bus replacement

California Energy Commission

Co-curricular activities

Contracting for service

Fee schedule

Preventive maintenance

Transportation fees

Transportation routing

Transportation scheduling

Walking distances

Discussion/Essay Questions

1. Student transportation has an enviable safety record. What are the major factors/safeguards that have contributed to this record?

2. A school board should consider a number of policy questions when planning or reviewing student transportation. Discuss three major issues that should be addressed in board policy.

3. Student transportation can be a major expense for a school district. Discuss three components of an efficient system designed to contain costs.

4. Student transportation fees have become increasingly common in California school districts. What are the pros and cons of charging student transportation fees?

Maintenance and Operations

CHAPTER

13

There is a strong and direct connection between the condition of a school building and a child's ability to learn.

(Bob Chase, President, National Education Association)

Introduction

School facilities are a major investment of citizens of the United States. Most communities take great pride in the appearance of their schools. Often, in fact, a community is judged by its schools. This judgment may be directly related to the academic accomplishments of students, but architectural design, campus cleanliness, and landscaping of school grounds also influence newcomers' judgments of a community's priorities for education.

The physical appearance of the school building is often a home buyer's first evidence of the quality of a district's schools. If schools are judged excellent and inspire community pride, real estate brokers often include this information in their advertising; they also may feature photographs of school sites. Besides offering these advantages in public relations, a well-designed school plant, carefully maintained and neatly kept, directly affects student and staff pride in a campus and exerts a strong influence on student learning.

Definitions

Although the words "maintenance" and "operations" are used interchangeably in many school districts, the terms are distinctly different. The maintenance department repairs and replaces buildings and equipment. Repair and replacement of floors, roofs, heating, air conditioning equipment, and broken windows are examples of maintenance. Replanting of lawns, shrubs, trees, and ground cover should be included in the maintenance budget, as should replacement of a sprinkler system. Maintenance keeps the grounds, buildings, and equipment in their original condition through repairs or through replacement with property of equal value and efficiency. If additional value and increased efficiency result from replacements, these additional values should be charged to capital outlay and credited to capital assets.

Operations, on the other hand, include the district's housekeeping routines that keep school plants functional. Operations are regular ongoing tasks that make schools ready for daily use. Operational expenses include utilities and the cleaning of classrooms and facilities. The operations budget also includes gardening, lawn-mowing, moving furniture, setting up a cafeteria, and delivering supplies to classrooms and offices.

Maintenance personnel are essentially repairpeople and may be called simply the "maintenance staff." In larger districts they have specific titles such as electrician, plumber, or carpenter. The operational staff are the housekeepers and cleaners; they commonly have job titles like janitor or custodian.

Board and District Policies

Every district is advised to adopt board policies regarding its maintenance and operations functions. These policies should include a philosophical statement that provides the community and staff with a vision of board priorities for maintaining and operating schools and should address the following questions:

Shall it be the philosophy of the district to maintain buildings and equipment in the same state of repair as homes and businesses in the district? A commitment in this area empowers the staff to plan a painting schedule, a calendar for re-roofing, and a timetable for replacement of equipment.

What type of financial commitment shall the district make to maintenance and operations? This dollar commitment may be calculated as an item-by-item budget for replacement and repair—or as a percentage of the budget with adjustments from year to year for unusual expenses. Unfortunately, in many California districts, as budget cutbacks have become necessary, maintenance and operations allocations have been severely reduced. Ultimately, if buildings and equipment are to return to a high degree of efficiency, taxpayers will face costs accumulated through years of neglect. From a public relations standpoint, it is sometimes difficult to convince taxpayers that a freshly-painted building, a well-manicured lawn, or a smoothly-paved driveway is a good investment.

What shall be the district's philosophy regarding contract maintenance work versus work completed by the district maintenance staff? Work handled by outside contractors means less work, and hence fewer positions, for the district's classified staff. Consequently, contracting out versus in-house work has become a major concern with classified unions and the legislature.

Routine repairs such as minor plumbing and electrical work, repair of minor roof leaks, broken windows, and the like are generally recognized as functions of district maintenance staff. However, depending on the size of the district and the equipment and specializations in the maintenance department, a district may find it advisable and less costly to contract for major repairs. A policy on this subject avoids untold grief and perhaps considerable expense.

What involvement shall the district maintenance staff have in capital improvement projects? The maintenance staffs often prefer "building projects." Erecting a new facility is more exciting than routine tasks like oiling the air-conditioning equipment or repairing a leaky roof. Nevertheless, a district maintenance staff is employed for just those routine purposes. Capital improvement ventures, on the other hand, typically require large work crews and special equipment. The maintenance staff should not undertake these major projects, thus inevitably neglecting work and increasing repair and replacement costs in the long run.

What shall be the priorities for responding to maintenance requests? The highest priority should be given to items that create a safety problem. Examples include a wiring condition that could give a severe electrical shock to an employee or student, or cracks in asphalt that could result in a playground accident.

Work that is not completed in timely fashion negatively affects classroom instruction and student and staff morale. Therefore, second priority should be given to "necessity for instruction." Examples include repair of dysfunctional equipment in a vocational shop class or a computer lab. The third priority would encompass those items, aesthetic in nature, that enhance the appearance of a campus, but do not relate directly to instruction. Reseeding a lawn and remodeling an office fall in this category.

What is the board's direction regarding such duties as cleaning of facilities and landscaping? For example, should a classroom be cleaned each day—or every other day? Given the emphasis in California on water and energy conservation, should lawns be maintained only for play spaces, with other areas planted in low-maintenance species? Or should schools preserve beautifully landscaped rose gardens that require considerable care? How shall such an addition to the aesthetic environment of a school be weighed against other budget requirements?

A policy in this area also gives direction to the director of maintenance and a school principal when citizens wish to donate a facility, trees, or other plants. It supports administrators in declining donations with little monetary value, but significant implications for maintenance and upkeep.

What is the organization plan for the maintenance and operations department? Board policy should establish an organizational chart that clearly delineates the chain of command and defines specific areas of responsibility for this department. This topic is discussed in greater detail in the next section.

A board that comes to grips with the above topics is better able to engage in long-range planning for facilities. Moreover, such policies increase the likelihood of convincing staff and the public of the district's need for funds to maintain facilities.

Organization

Organization of maintenance and operations departments varies from district to district. Because the maintenance department has districtwide responsibilities, staff members are usually responsible to a director of maintenance. The director is a line administrator who reports in turn to the district business manager. In smaller districts, however, the director may be directly responsible to the superintendent.

Organizational patterns for operations departments are even more diverse. Some district organizational charts show this employee group directly responsible to a building principal; others, to a director of maintenance. In the former case, the director serves in a staff relationship as an advisor to employees and the principal.

The following principles should be considered when developing an organizational chart for the maintenance and operations department.

- The organizational chart should be approved by the governing board
- Lines of authority should be clearly delineated, showing the direct supervisor for each position or group of positions
- All employees should be responsible only to one direct supervisor, because overlapping of supervisory personnel leads to confusion and misunderstandings
- Job descriptions should be developed for each job classification and should clearly state the supervisor for that classification.

Maintenance and Operations Budget

Comments appear on the preceding pages about the necessity of an adequate budget for maintenance and upkeep of facilities and equipment. In most districts the budget for this department is exceeded only by certificated personnel costs.

Adherence to the following guidelines assists administrative staff and the board in budgeting properly for this department.

Replacement and Repair of Equipment and Facilities

Each district should develop a master plan for equipment replacement and repair. The master plan should identify critical points for each year and should encompass at least a five-year period. The life span of roofs, plumbing, electrical equipment, boilers, and other major cost items should be plotted and dealt with on a year-by-year basis. The master plan reduces emergency repairs. It avoids large, unplanned expenses that will inevitably occur if an accumulation of roofs, plumbing systems, or other capital outlay items were to need replacement in the same year.

Work Orders

The director of maintenance should establish a work order system to account for repairs efficiently. Most districts use a computer to track and cost out each work order. This information is used to project budget needs for succeeding years.

Personnel Costs

Procedures for determining personnel costs range from estimating labor on each work order to a yearly determination of the department's budget for salaries and benefits. In most districts, tracking labor costs for each job is unnecessary. Nevertheless, the director must ensure that tasks are completed in an efficient and timely fashion. In addition, personnel costs for future years must be accurately projected.

End-of-Year Balance

It is extremely important that the business manager monitor closely the expenditures in maintenance and operations. Many business managers have been embarrassed, and others dismissed from their positions, for failing to do so. An unexpected need to replace a boiler at a cost of more than $40,000 can exceed budget allocations in a hurry.

All personnel costs should be encumbered at the beginning of the year so the business and department managers know how much money will be available after all salaries and benefits have been paid. Close attention should be paid to approval of overtime, substitutes, and extra duty hours. A precise system for controlling these costs is essential.

Reserve Fund

Since it is virtually impossible to predict the life span of every piece of equipment or the timing of certain repairs, a reserve fund for the unforeseen is a good budget practice. This account should be clearly designated and its purpose communicated to the staff. Some employee groups have accused business managers of "hiding money" by overestimating maintenance and operations budgets, thus tying up funds that could have been available for salaries. Highlighting the need for a maintenance reserve fund and informing staff and citizens of its purpose help to alleviate this concern.

SUMMARY

Attractive, functional, and well-maintained school facilities are often perceived as indicators of an excellent school district. Schools are a source of student, parent, and community pride and deserve to be well maintained. This task is properly the function of the district's maintenance and operations department.

A district that adopts a philosophy and a long-range plan for maintenance and preservation of its campuses clearly establishes a sound organizational design for the department. As a rule, where maintenance and operations funds are prudently provided and monitored, the community perceives its schools as a good investment and education as a high priority.

KEY TERMS

Board policies	Lines of authority
Capital improvement projects	Maintenance
Contract maintenance	Maintenance staff
Direct supervision	Operations
End-of-year balance	Replacement of equipment
Energy conservation	Reserve Fund
Housekeeping	Work orders

Discussion/Essay Questions

1. An argument can be made that a well-maintained and attractive school has educational benefits for students. Do you agree or disagree? What priority should be placed on the budget for maintenance and operations?

2. "Maintenance" and "operations" are two words that are often used interchangeably. Discuss the differences between the two terms.

3. Board policies establish priorities for the total educational enterprise. Discuss three topics for inclusion in board policies that would establish a board's priority for maintenance and operations.

4. The budget for maintenance and operations may be a significant percentage of a district budget. How should the maintenance and operations department be organized for maximum efficiency?

CHAPTER 14

School Food Service Program

*The first duty of government is to see that people have food, fuel, and clothes.
The second, that they have means of moral and intellectual education.*

(John Ruskin, in Fors Clavigera, *1876)*

Introduction

The British scholar and artist John Ruskin wrote a series of letters, known as *Fors Clavigera*, to the workmen and laborers of Great Britain (Ruskin Programme, n.d.). Perhaps the above quotation from one of those letters inspired the U.S. Congress and President Truman to approve the National School Lunch Program in 1946. Most educators would subscribe to the thought that it is very difficult to teach a hungry child and that the federal and state lunch and breakfast programs have made the task of teaching a child much easier.

Thus, providing a nutritious meal for school children has become national policy and a major management task for school administrators. This chapter contains a brief history of the food service program, information about the National School Lunch and Breakfast Programs, and discussion of the educational value of providing school food service. The national problem of obesity and health-related problems is reviewed, along with requirements for district participation in the food service programs. The chapter concludes with information for school administrators who manage the program and some thoughts on the future of food service.

History of the Food Service Program

The beginning of concern for student nutrition can be traced to 1790 in Germany when Count Rumsford organized soup kitchens to feed the hungry children of Germany (Caton, 1990). Other European countries followed Germany's example, and programs spread throughout much of Europe during the 19th and 20th centuries.

The earliest known program in the U.S. was established in New York City in 1853 by the Children's Aid Society. The society prepared and served meals for children who attended a vocational school. Over the next several decades various private organizations established food service programs in several cities, including Boston, Philadelphia, Cincinnati, and St. Louis.

In 1904 Robert Hunter's book, *Poverty*, was published. Hunter attributed the lack of learning among poor children to hunger. He estimated that there were 60,000 to 70,000 children in New York City who arrived at school each day too hungry to complete their schoolwork. This widely read book inspired many private and public institutions to establish food programs for the poor.

As early as 1921, the Los Angeles Board of Education established a food service program in nine high schools, eight intermediate schools, and 31 elementary schools. Student body organizations or a cafeteria director selected by the home economics department managed the secondary programs. Elementary programs were managed by the Parent Teacher Association (PTA). Lunches were sold at cost, but students who were unable to pay were given a free lunch. The PTA made up any deficit for elementary students, and secondary students were given jobs at the school to pay for their lunch (Gunderson, 2004).

During the depression years of the 1930s, poverty and hunger greatly increased in the United States. Malnutrition and hunger were widely documented in books and in the newly invented motion picture. John Steinbeck's *Grapes of Wrath* (1939) depicted the suffering and hunger of good people trying to cope and maintain some sense of dignity during that period of time.

After the U.S. entered World War II, the War Department documented the necessity of rejecting prospective draftees because of malnutrition. Thus, it was seen in the best interest of the country that children receive at least one balanced meal per day. The National School Lunch Act of 1946 was a consequence of that belief.

Young People's Eating Habits: A Call for Change

Numerous studies report an alarming increase among young people of childhood obesity and other health risks such as diabetes and high blood pressure. The U.S. Department of Agriculture's Center for Nutrition Policy and Promotion reported in 1999 that the diet quality of most American children needs improvement. The Center reported that 88% of children have a diet that is inadequate.

Junk food, caffeine, and soda consumption are particular areas of concern. A paper entitled "Liquid Candy" reported that consumption of soft drinks among teens in 1996 was approximately double that of 20 years earlier. Over that same time period, milk consumption *decreased* in a similar proportion. Soft drinks give teen-agers the equivalent of 10 to 15 teaspoons of sugar daily (Jacobson, 1998). A more recent survey of more than 500 fourth-graders in Maryland found that 20% of these children skipped breakfast or lunch at least four days a week (Gross, 2004). Another recent report (Collins, 2004) found that soft drinks and junk food accounted for more than 30% of teen-agers' diets, with concomitant deficits in essential vitamins and minerals.

Several states, including California, have taken steps to provide healthier meals for students. Texas banned junk food in it elementary and middle schools. New York City banned junk food from all school vending machines. In 2002, Los Angeles Unified School District banned the sale of soft drinks in district schools. The district also took action to eliminate fried chips, candy, and other junk foods from school vending machines and student stores, and to place a strict limit on the amount of fat, sugar, and sodium in any snacks sold during the school day.

In 2003, the California Legislature and Governor also took positive steps to promote healthy nutrition. Senate Bill 677, The California Childhood Obesity Prevention Act became effective January 1, 2004. The objective of the legislation is to reduce the amount of soft drinks consumed by students. SB 677 prohibits school districts from selling soft drinks to students during the school day. The legislature presented the following findings in support of the new restrictions:

- In the past two decades obesity has doubled in children and tripled in adolescents
- On average, 30% of California's children are overweight; in some districts this number ranges up to 50%
- Only 2% of California students aged 12 to 17 have eating habits that meet national dietary recommendations
- Only 23% of pupils in grades 5, 7, and 9 are physically fit
- Overweight and physical inactivity cost California an estimated $24.6 billion annually, approximately $750 per person
- Poor nutrition and physical inactivity account for more preventable deaths (28%) than anything other than tobacco—more than AIDS, violence, car crashes, alcohol, and drugs combined
- Each additional serving of sugar-sweetened soda increases a child's risk for obesity by 60%.

This legislation allows only water, milk, and fruit-based drinks containing 50% fruit juice with no added sweeteners. At secondary schools one additional drink is permitted: an electrolyte replacement beverage that contains no more than 42 grams of added sweetener per 20 oz. serving. The only exception is that elementary schools may permit the sale of "forbidden" items as part of a fundraising event if students sell the items and the sale is off school premises. The sale must also be more than one hour after the end of the school day. Secondary students have a bit more latitude as the sale may occur during a school-sponsored event after the school day. Sales may also occur in vending machines, student stores, and cafeterias one half-hour after the school day.

Good Nutrition and Student Achievement

Health educators, nutritionists, and physical education experts point to study after study showing that good nutrition programs result in better classroom achievement and higher academic performance (Saunders, Fee, & Gottlieb, 1999). Nevertheless, many of the state's public school students receive no nutrition guidelines, eat fast-food lunches served by the cafeteria, and successfully avoid physical education programs. School nutrition experts estimate that one-half of the student population routinely skips breakfast and makes up a quarter of their daily meals from junk food.

The National Center for Chronic Disease Prevention and Health Promotion (2003) reported data from 1999 showing that 76% of high school students were not eating the recommended amount of fruits and vegetables. Another federal report, *America's Children: Key National Indicators of Well-Being 2003* (Federal Interagency, 2003), found that only 20% of two- to six-year-olds were following a good diet, a number that decreased to 8% by the time those children were teenagers. The same report showed that the percentage of children aged 6 to 18 who were overweight rose from 6% in 1980 to 15% in 1999–2000.

Several national studies have linked nutritious school breakfast programs with academic achievement. In Minnesota and Massachusetts, students who participated in a school breakfast program showed improvement in reading and math scores on tests of basic skills. A Baltimore study showed that skipping breakfast even once a week negatively affected students' problem-solving ability that day (Jeffers, 2000).

A 2001 California study matched fitness scores on the state-mandated physical fitness test and student scores in reading and math on the Stanford Achievement Test. The key findings included:

- Higher achievement was associated with higher levels of fitness at the fifth, seventh, and ninth grades
- Students who met minimum fitness levels in three or more physical fitness areas showed the greatest gains in academic achievement at all three grade levels (Winger, 2002).

National School Lunch Program (NSLP)

The National School Lunch Program was signed into law by Harry Truman in 1946 and was considered one of the most significant accomplishments of his presidency. The program was an outstanding success; within one year, a half billion meals had been prepared and served to 7.1 million children (American School Food Service Association, 2004).

The philosophy underlying the program stressed health and nutrition. The overriding concern was taking care of the basic nutritional needs of students so they could focus on their studies, rather than hunger pangs. Another factor behind the legislation was the availability of surplus commodities, which are provided to schools by the federal government to supplement commercially purchased food supplies. Thus, the act provided an incentive to school districts in the form of surplus farm supplies and a small cash reimbursement.

Providing food to children has remained national policy, with the result that today, almost 100,000 public schools serve more than 31 million students a daily meal that meets dietary guidelines established by the National School lunch program. Over one-half, 21 million, of these children receive free or reduced-price lunches (Food Research and Action Center, 2014).

In 2010, President Obama signed the Healthy, Hunger-Free Kids Act of 2010. This act provides funds for the school lunch program until 2015. The law increased for the first time in 15 years reimbursement to schools for the lunch and breakfast programs- the increase was six cents per meal. Schools are required to meet nutrition standards for school breakfast, lunches and snacks, and eliminate junk food sold a la carte or from vending machines.

The First Lady, Michelle Obama, campaigned for a new simpler image of a healthy meal called MyPlate. It replaces the food pyramid and is split into four sections: fruit, vegetables, grains, and protein. A smaller circle is for dairy products (Steffen, 2010).

After the Obama rules took effect some districts reported a drop in the number of children participating in the breakfast and lunch programs. There were also reports of more food dumped in the trash. The children said that the food was not as tasty, and some critics blamed the stricter standards for fat, sugar, and vegetable consumption as the reason for fewer students eating in the school cafeteria (Severson, 2017).

California's School Lunch Program

The California Department of Education, Nutrition Services Division, administers California's food service program. Food service in California schools is big business. California provides approximately 10% of the school lunches served in the United States. On an average day in California, more than 4.7 million meals are served at approximately 43,000 locations. The California Department of Education (CDE,2011) disburses approximately $1.65 billion in federal and state funds to eligible agencies to provide meals.

There is widespread public misconception that most students participate in the program. In reality, only 70 percent of eligible California students participated in the school lunch program during the 2009–2010 school year and participation in the breakfast program was even lower, 30 percent (Lin, 2011).

All California schools must meet the USDA nutritional requirements for the school lunch program. For children ages 6–12, minimum requirements include:

- 1 cup fluid whole milk or approved alternative
- 2 oz. of meat or meat alternative (e.g., poultry, fish, cheese, eggs, dry beans or peas, peanut butter, other nut butters, or yogurt)
- 3/4 cup juice or two or more fruits or vegetables
- 1 slice or 1/2 cup serving of enriched or whole-grain bread or bread alternative (rolls, muffins, noodles, rice, etc.) (CDE, 2011).

In addition, no more than 30% of a student's calories can come from fat, and less than 10% from saturated fat. The lunch must provide one-third of the recommended daily amounts of vitamin A, vitamin C, iron, and calcium (Food Research, 2004b).

School Breakfast Program (SBP)

Another phase of food services, the School Breakfast Program, was established by an Act of Congress in 1966. Congress recognized that many students were going hungry during the school day, with an adverse educational effect. In particular, many students in rural communities travel long distances to school each day. The breakfast program was originally designed to meet the needs of these children. It was piloted under the Federal Child Nutrition Act of 1966. Subsequently, the program was expanded to all public and nonprofit schools, as well as to residential childcare institutions.

As a federal program, the School Breakfast Program is administered in much the same fashion as the lunch program. Both programs must be open to all students. If a child qualifies for free or reduced-price lunches, then the student also qualifies for free or reduced-price breakfasts.

All California schools must meet the federal nutritional requirements for the breakfast program. For children aged 6 to 12, these include:

- 1 cup fluid milk
- 1/2 cup of fruit, vegetable, or fruit or vegetable juice
- one of the following options:
    1 slice of whole grain or enriched bread
    1 serving of cornbread, biscuit, roll, or muffin
    1/2 cup of cooked cereal, pasta, or noodles (Food and Nutrition, 2003).

District Reimbursement

The lunch and breakfast programs are federal programs that assist schools in providing breakfast and lunch for students at a reasonable price. The U.S. Department of Agriculture is responsible for managing and supervising the national program. Both public and private schools are eligible to participate in the program. Participating schools receive cash subsidies and donated commodities from the U.S. Department of Agriculture for each meal they serve. School districts can also be reimbursed for snacks served in after-school programs.

Hungry Children—Free and Reduced-Price Meals

By all measures, the United States is the wealthiest country in the world. Therefore, it might seem surprising that hunger exists among the population. In 2012, the U.S. Department of Agriculture estimated that 85% of American households had enough food for an active life. The USDA uses the term "food insecure" for families who do not have enough food. The department estimates that almost 15% of families went hungry at least part of the time during that year.

California Education Code Section 49550 requires all public school districts and county superintendents of schools to make available, free or at a reduced price, one meal to each needy student every school day. A needy student is one who qualifies under established guidelines. The following were guidelines for 2014–2015:

- Children from families that receive food stamps are automatically eligible for free meals.
- A foster care child who is the legal responsibility of the welfare agency or ward of the court.
- If family income (household of four) earns less than $45,510 per year (CDE, 2017).

Each school district establishes the charge for breakfast and lunch. Therefore, there is a slight variation in the cost by districts. For example, in 2017-2018 the cost of breakfast in the Santa Monica School District was $1.25 while it was $1.75 in the Oceanside District. Lunch was $2.00 in Oceanside and $3.50 in Santa Monica. The reader can go to the website for California school districts where the cost of meals is posted.

As of this writing, President Trump's plan for the nation's school service program is still in the development stage. The president's initial plan called for a 21 percent reduction of the department of agriculture's budget, which could curtail funds for the food service program. The president has often spoken of the need for the reduction of federal rules and regulations and time will tell what effect that issue could have on the school breakfast and lunch program (Severson, 2017).

Organization of the Food Service Program

In most districts, the assistant superintendent of business services or the chief business officer has direct responsibility for the food service department. The business officer usually has a director of food services to maintain control over the program. The director has responsibility for daily operations, purchasing, and budgeting, as well as menu planning. Because the state and federal governments supply funds for the program, it is imperative that the director accurately track all income and expenditures. Food service monies are placed in a restricted fund that program directors strive to keep self-supporting.

Some districts operate a kitchen at each school. Others distribute food to satellite locations from one or more central food processing centers. Still other districts contract with private companies to provide breakfast and lunch.

Keeping the School Food Service Program Self-Supporting

One of the major challenges that food service directors face is keeping the food service program on a self-supporting basis. In the past, many districts used the General Fund to help food service programs make it to the end of the year—but no more. The two major expenses in a food service program are personnel and food. In recent years energy costs have also increased expenditures for food services. Food directors must review each of these factors to make a food service program support itself.

Personnel Costs

Districts have typically paid all personnel costs from the food service restricted fund. However, the General Fund has occasionally "bailed out" this fund by paying for such items as fringe benefits. But what about support personnel who spend a portion of their time on cafeteria-related duties? A portion of salaries could be paid for the following services: purchasing food, processing invoices, paying invoices, preparing and processing payroll, repairing food service equipment, cleaning the cafeteria, and removing trash and garbage.

One way to avoid overstaffing is to calculate the meals served per labor hour. To complete this calculation, it is necessary to develop a formula to equate à la carte food items with meals. To keep careful track of the food service program, many districts generate a monthly profit-and-loss statement for each school. This statement reports expenses and revenues so schools can track their status from month to month.

Supplies and Equipment

The keys to controlling food cost are to hold inventory at its lowest feasible level, to avoid waste, and to restrict use of high-cost food items. Achieving these objectives depends upon accurate records and strict adherence to food inventory procedures. Money can usually be saved by combining government commodity food—whether meats, grains, or vegetables—with other ingredients and presenting food items that students enjoy. To control costs, many districts have completely eliminated high-cost food items. For example, one district temporarily eliminated pizza from the menu when cheese was not received as a commodity from the government.

Legitimate Food Service Fund expenditures include new equipment, equipment repair and replacement, and detergent and cleaning supplies. Telephone, postage, and pest control costs may also be charged to the Food Service Fund.

Energy Costs

The district should monitor carefully both gas and electric consumption for meal preparation. With increased rates for electricity, converting an all-electric kitchen to natural gas may be a good investment. The cost of an efficiency audit of air conditioning and refrigeration units may also be money well spent. For example, one high school significantly reduced operating costs by installing two air-conditioning chillers, one large and one small, in place of a single super chiller.

Energy costs may be reduced by structuring the time of meal preparation so expensive energy time periods may be avoided. Otherwise, energy use in school buildings is highest from late morning to early afternoon, rather than at any other time during the day, largely because of immense energy consumption through food preparation.

Donated Commodities

The commodities program supplies food to schools in two ways. The first, which makes up a majority of the food served, is called "entitlement commodities." Schools choose these commodities, and the U.S. Department of Agriculture purchases them to send to the schools. These commodities include flour, oil, ground beef, chicken, turkey, canned peaches and pears, and tuna.

The second category is "bonus" or "surplus commodities." These are purchased by the U.S. government when farmers produce so much of an item that sales on the open market would not yield enough to keep them in business. The government buys the surplus to keep prices steady. Most farm products are the same products, such as milk and cheese, that schools use continuously in their food service program.

For the past few years there has been a reduction in federally donated commodities, forcing an increase in district expenditures for food. This increase has, in turn, reduced the ability of many districts, even those with high free and reduced-price meal eligibility, to operate a completely self-supporting program. Another factor that may influence the commodities program is trade agreements that the U.S. has signed, e.g., the North American Free Trade Agreement and the General Agreement on Tariffs and Trade. These agreements may offset the availability of commodities and affect their cost.

Increased Revenues

To increase food sales, the food service director, principal, and staff must focus on the client—the student. Competition for students' dollars by off-campus restaurants, student body sales, and other fund-raising activities forces administrators to active marketing of school nutrition programs. Quality customer service is the best way to market the food service program. Like any business, school food service must be customer-oriented to succeed.

Successful programs involve students in selecting menus and recipes. Food courts and an á la carte line for quick service have greatly increased student participation in the school lunch program. At secondary schools, salads, pizza, baked potatoes, hamburgers, tacos, and soup have become staples.

Members of the Associated Student Body can play key roles in promoting the food service program. Students are influenced by their peers, particularly at the secondary school level; thus, if student leaders are supportive of the food service program, a major step will have been taken toward encouraging students to eat lunch in the cafeteria. The successful food service director spends time with teenagers, observing the latest trends and interests, to design a program that responds to their preferences.

To encourage elementary students to eat school lunches, the food service director must first motivate students to become interested in the cafeteria. The principal and food service director can create this interest by inventive menu descriptions, contests, and occasionally inviting parents to join the students at lunch in the cafeteria.

Attention must also be directed to promoting participation by members of the school staff. For instance, many schools have designed attractive dining areas for the staff. Teachers should also be given opportunity to request menus and to suggest strategies to encourage students to eat lunch on campus.

Trends in Food Services

District food service programs are big business. As such, they experience many of the same ups and downs as other businesses. Reductions in funds and commodity donations from state and federal governments have forced food service programs to consider several changes. Since students can easily access commercial fast foods, school food programs have begun to offer more à la carte selections and in greater variety. To this end, food carts and specialty centers are on the increase; they extend advertising for the food service program beyond the cafeteria. Many schools attract students to the cafeteria by playing music in the serving area. Others keep students on campus by holding pep rallies and other school events during the lunch period.

Some schools have turned to fast food and soda companies, like Del Taco and Burger King, for part of the daily meals. Cafeteria managers have found that children will eat at school more often if fast food is available. Although these meals may not be the most nutritious, they increase the likelihood that children are eating at least something.

Districts across the nation are working to improve food service. Los Angeles School District is an example; the district feeds 650,000 students each day. Eighty percent of the students qualify for free or reduced price breakfast and lunch. Some schools are serving a vegan lunch and an afternoon meal, called "supper."

In 2017 the district was the sponsor of Senate Bill 557, which was designed to help solve the problem of uneaten food left over in the cafeterias each day. A 2015 study by the Los Angeles District showed that schools were throwing out 600 tons of uneaten food a week, much of it milk. This law gives the schools the right to give leftover food to food banks and charities. Leftovers include unopened milk cartons and uncut fruit (Boessenkool, 2017).

SUMMARY

This nation recognized more than a half a century ago the importance of providing at least one nutritious meal a day for school children. The National Food Service Program has continued to expand with greater participation by the nation's schools since its origin in 1946. Each year, a greater number of students depend on the school cafeteria to provide their breakfast and lunch.

Surprisingly to many, a substantial number of children come to school hungry each day, even though obesity is on the rise among children and adolescents. The nation has increasingly become concerned with the problem of poor nutrition and the subsequent health issues associated with that problem. Many states, school districts, and food service managers have been at the forefront in attempting to provide more nutritious meals in school cafeterias and to educate students to a more healthful lifestyle.

School superintendents and cafeteria managers must balance the need to provide healthful and nutritious meals with budget constraints. Food service directors are continually forced to ensure that their feeding programs are self-supporting and not a drain on the General Fund. An effective manager organizes the food service program to encourage maximum participation by students and staff and economizes on expenses by keeping a watchful eye on personnel and energy costs. Menus that maximize the use of donated commodities also reduce expenditures.

A number of trends in the food service arena are emerging with a greater focus on nutrition and health issues leading the way. Some of the predicted trends include:

- Greater attention will be given to nutrition education and encouragement of healthful eating habits among the student clientele
- Food courts will become a common practice, particularly in secondary schools
- Serving fresh fruits and vegetables will become more common
- Modern technology will play a larger role in food preparation and management of the program

KEY TERMS

Central kitchen

Child Nutrition Act of 1966

Contracted services

Donated commodities

Energy costs

Lunch components

NSLP

Nutrition requirements

Personnel costs

Reimbursements

School Breakfast Program

School Lunch Act of 1946

Senate Bill 557

Serving lines

State Meal Program

U.S. Department of Agriculture

Discussion/Essay Questions

1. Discuss recent trends in school food service programs. What are the benefits and drawbacks of these trends?

2. Child nutrition programs are jointly sponsored by federal, state, and local government. What is the role of each level of government in the child nutrition program?

3. The school food service program is designed to ensure that students receive a well-balanced meal. What are the nutritional requirements of the school lunch program?

4. Most school districts attempt to operate the food service program so that it is financially self-supporting. Discuss three important factors that must be considered to achieve this objective.

CHAPTER 15

Facilities: A California Challenge

We are confident that California voters remain willing to invest in education and the future of the state and our children.

(Carla Niño, President of California Parent Teacher Association, December 2003)

Introduction

The education debate has centered primarily on student learning, but a secondary issue is school facilities—the need for additional classrooms and for school maintenance and upgrades. The National Center for Educational Statistics (NCES, 2017) estimates that K-12 school enrollment will reach almost 51 million students in 2017-2018, and is projected to increase to 58 million in 2025. Increases are expected in the South and West, and decreases are expected in the Northeast and Midwest.

The states and nation will be challenged to provide facilities for the additional seven million students expected in the next eight years. In addition to the requirement for new facilities there is an urgent need for modernization and upgrading of older facilities. Earlier in this text, there was a brief discussion of President Trump's plan for upgrading the nation's infrastructure. The reader should closely follow news reports of the president's plan for schools.

The American Society of Civil Engineers reports that many of the nation's schools are suffering from neglect—poor ventilation, energy problems and mold. The Civil Engineers gave school facilities a "D" grade.

As discussed in previous chapters, California student enrollment is starting to decline. However, that decline is uneven among the 1000 school districts with enrollment increasing in some districts and declining in others. During the decades of growth, most districts met the need for additional housing by adding portable classrooms, but the aged portables cannot be easily moved to those districts that are experiencing growth.

In addition to the need for new facilities, pressure to upgrade facilities is mounting nation-wide. This statement is particularly true in California. In 2000, the American Civil Liberties Union (ACLU) filed a lawsuit, *Williams v. California*, charging California with responsibility for substandard conditions in its urban schools. The ACLU based its suit on a five-month study of education in California. The study included interviews with parents, students, and teachers. Among the many charges filed in the suit, the most pertinent regarding school facilities include:

- There are no specific standards requiring public schools to provide heat in winter
- There are no clear state requirements that schools have functioning toilets
- There is no regulation to protect students from infestations by rats and cockroaches ("ACLU," 2000).

A series of bills were approved by the legislature in 2006 to implement and add to the settlement made by the ACLU and the governor. The bills included procedures for emergency repairs at schools and standards for school facilities. In addition, the legislation requires districts to develop a complaint process and gives county superintendents greater responsibility for oversight of districts in each county.

History of Funding for Facilities

Lack of facilities is not a new problem. California has experienced steady growth in student population with consequent need for new schools ever since it became a state in 1850. Finance for school facilities has passed through three distinct phases. Phase one began with adoption of the California Constitution and ended in the years following World War II. During this phase the cost of school construction was borne by the taxpayers in local school districts. The key to success was local voter approval to issue General Obligation Bonds (GO Bonds) in an amount up to 5% of assessed property valuation (10% in unified districts). More than half of all present facilities were built during that time.

During phase two, from the end of World War II to the passage of Proposition 13 in 1978, GO Bonds were still the primary vehicle for funding school construction. However, many school districts were swamped with growth in student enrollment during that period and reached the limit of their bonding capacity. Consequently, the state entered the school construction arena in the late 1940s, on an emergency basis, and granted help to some of the most impacted districts. This stopgap effort led to adoption in 1952 of a state school building program under which the state legislature implemented construction aid to school districts that continued for 26 years, until 1978.

Under this plan the first responsibility was placed on the local school district, which had to bond itself to capacity. Once bonding capacity was reached, the state advanced enough funds to house the projected student population. These funds were loaned to districts, to be paid back to the state by formula over 30 to 40 years. By this method, the state used its credit to extend the credit of the local district. The formula included an equalization factor in that low-wealth districts were the first to participate in the state program. Districts with greater resources were expected to continue to fund school construction without state aid. This program worked well until 1978.

Phase three started after the passage of Proposition 13 in 1978. Since then, property taxes have been limited to 1% of assessed valuation. General Obligation (GO) Bonds, with redemption supported by a local *ad valorem* tax, were no longer possible. This limitation reduced school districts' ability to raise funds for any purpose, including facilities construction. Therefore, to continue to build schools, the state assumed a major role in construction financing.

School districts were unable to use GO Bonds for school construction for an eight-year period, from 1978 to 1986. Then, in 1986, Proposition 46 was approved by California voters, restoring to school districts the authority to seek voter approval for bond issues. Nevertheless, the state continued as the major source of funds for school construction. This circumstance stemmed largely from the state's ability to pass a bond issue by simple majority, whereas districts were required to obtain approval of 2/3 of voters. In the year 2000, however, a voter initiative reduced the 2/3 requirement to 55%.

The 55% requirement has enabled local school districts to pass a greater number of bond elections. For example, there were 63 bond elections for school facilities in March of 2004. Of the 63, only 15 would have passed with the 66-2/3% requirement. But at a 55% level, 53 (84%) of the measures were approved. However, ten districts were unable to reach even the 55% level (CASH, 2004).

Finance and Facilities

The state's capital investment in school buildings is massive. California has approximately 9,903 schools and 303,399 classrooms. Seventy-one percent of the classrooms are more than 25 years old. The California Department of Education estimates that more than 4,000 new classrooms are needed each year, or 12 per day to meet the increase in student enrollment. There is also a need to modernize 20 classrooms per day. The department estimates the cost of new construction and modernization at greater than $11 billion over a five-year period (CDE, 2010).

At the present time the major means of financing school construction dollars is a bond issue approved by voters. Typically, the state makes principal and interest payments on bonds over a period of 20 years. Revenues for these payments come from state income taxes, sales taxes, and corporate profit taxes.

Statewide bond measures can be placed on the state ballot in the June or November election of even-numbered years. State bond propositions require a simple majority for passage. From 1998 through 2006 California citizens approved 36 billion for school construction (CDE, 2007). The 2006 state bond was for $10.4 billion dollars. The ten billion was long spent before another state bond was approved ten years later in 2016, Proposition 51. It was for $9 billion to fund construction and improvement of school facilities (Buechley, 2017).

In the face of burgeoning demands for remodeling and construction, local school boards, state officials, and the educational community have created a variety of strategies to finance school construction. The major strategies are discussed in the following paragraphs.

School Building Lease/Purchase Programs— Leroy Greene Funds

The Leroy Greene Lease/Purchase program makes funds available for school construction when funding eligibility requirements are met. Eligibility is based on state-developed criteria that define inadequate student housing. The square footage allocation to districts is based on a policy established in the early 1950s and differs according to level—elementary, middle/junior high, or high school. Under this formula an average California classroom covers 960 square feet, among the smallest in the nation.

Leroy Greene funds may also purchase school sites. This allocation also differs by school grade levels. Generally, the state allocates a maximum of 10 acres for an elementary school, 20 acres for a middle or junior high school, and 40 acres for a high school site. Most educators agree that both the square footage and the acreage allocation are inadequate to the educational needs of students in the 21st century.

School districts are allocated monies according to a point system. As of January 1, 1987, districts must match from local monies the funds they receive from the state. Distribution of Leroy Greene monies for school construction is determined by the State Allocation Board (SAB). This seven-member group is composed of four members of the California legislature and one representative each from the Department of Finance, the Department of Education, and the Department of General Services. The SAB also leases relocatable classrooms to school districts and uses income from those leases to purchase more portable units.

Since funds are not available to meet the needs of every district within the state, districts are forced to compete with one another for available dollars. Districts applying for funds must justify their request, with the result that districts that are most skillful and energetic in their presentations often receive the funding. Many districts have employed lobbyists and school facility specialists in hopes of obtaining the maximum possible funds from the State Allocation Board. This factor places at a disadvantage those small districts with personnel and resources too limited for the employment of lobbyists or consultants. Finally, district administrators find it very frustrating to work through the process, meeting all eligibility requirements, only to discover that no money is available.

The state school facilities program also includes the Deferred Maintenance Fund, Asbestos Abatement Fund, and Incentive Program for Year-Round Schools. In the early 1980s tideland oil revenues supported the Leroy Greene program. However, the primary source of funds has become the sale of state General Obligation Bonds approved by voters, as discussed above.

Local Funding Options

Developer Fees

Developer fees levied on new residential and commercial construction provide another option to fund school construction. The School Financing Plan of 1986 authorized school districts to levy school facility fees on residential and commercial developers when new housing construction creates a need for new school facilities. Prior to 1986, developer fees for school construction varied widely throughout the state. Some school districts had no means of financing needed facilities, while others levied charges in excess of $10,000 per new home.

A 1986 law limited school construction fees on new residential development to $1.50 per square foot. Fees on commercial/industrial development were limited to 25 cents per square foot. An inflation factor, provided for in the law, allows the fee to increase each year. In 2017, the fee was $3.48 for residential and 56 cents for commercial/industrial development (San Diego School District, 2017).

Developer fees were originally conceived as a vehicle to provide interim housing for students. The mechanism by which developer fees are imposed depends upon a district showing that new housing creates a need for new schools. Having done so, the district has authority to establish developer fees as a condition of the issuance of building permits by the responsible government agency. Cities and counties may impose three types of fees on developers: impact fees (SB 201), city or county fees, and mitigation fees. Impact fees may be spent on interim facilities for a five-year period. Mitigation fees reduce the impact of housing developments on existing school facilities.

Developer-Donated Schools

A developer may legally donate a school to the district in lieu of paying developer fees. Should this occur, the advantage to the district is that all other fees may be eliminated. Unfortunately, this action is rarely taken by a developer.

Certificates of Participation (COPs)

School districts that can handle long-term debt have the option of issuing certificates of participation. COPs are similar to bonds in that they secure funding for capital projects by means of a promise to pay principal and interest to the investor over a period of time. They are not secured by a tax increase, as are General Obligation Bonds. These negotiable certificates are issued by a district indirectly, through a specially created nonprofit corporation and trustee. Certificates of participation are sold by an underwriter to investors. Because they are secured by the financial integrity of the school district rather than an increase in taxes, voter approval is not required, and income may be used to purchase either real or "personal" (equipment, etc.) property.

The COP debt must be serviced by the General Fund. When COPs are issued to finance new construction, the nonprofit corporation leases the building to the district, the district pays rent from its General Fund, and the investors have an undivided percentage interest in those lease payments. It is common for school districts to service their COP debt from developer fees. Districts may also sell or lease surplus property and apply that income to the annual COP obligation. Proceeds from a pass-through of Redevelopment Agency funds may also be used to pay the debt.

The payments on COPs are a primary demand on the revenues of school districts that elect this method of school funding. Thus, COPs are viable only for districts that foresee sufficient income to retire the debt. Many districts lack the resources necessary to back certificates in the amount needed to build schools.

Lottery Funds

Lottery funds may be used to purchase personal property and some real property and for remodeling. The same amendment to the state constitution that established the lottery also forbids expenditure of these funds for construction of new facilities. There is much confusion and misunderstanding among members of the general public about the amount of funds generated by the lottery—not even close to the amount needed for facilities construction—and about the ways in which those funds may be used.

Local General Obligation (GO) Bonds

Although local bond elections were eliminated by Proposition 13, they were reinstated in 1986 by passage of Proposition 46. This proposition was an important restoration of capital outlay funding ability to school districts. School districts could form special districts to sell construction bonds, subject to approval by 2/3 of the voters in the special district. Meanwhile, funds to repair or replace structurally unsafe buildings required approval by a simple majority of district voters.

Between 1986 (when authority of school districts to place GO Bonds on the ballot was restored) and 1999, some 450 bond issues were placed on a ballot. Of these, 243 received the required 2/3 approval, a rate of 54%. Had the vote requirement been a simple majority during this time, the success rate would have been a spectacular 94% ("Voters," 1999). Consequently, the educational community attempted several times to change the requirement for passage of a GO Bond measure from 2/3 to a simple majority vote. California citizens considered measures to make the change to a simple majority requirement in 1993 and again in the spring of 2000. Both attempts failed. As a compromise, the educational community agreed to place Proposition 39 on the fall 2000 ballot. This proposition, lowering the required vote from 2/3 to 55%, was approved by voters.

Voter approval allows a school or special district to sell bonds to be retired by imposing an *ad valorem* tax on the property tax rolls of the district. Bonds issued by the district represent a promise to pay principal and interest to the investors over a period of time limited to a maximum of 25 years. The bonds are popular with many investors, as the interest earned is tax-exempt at both state and federal levels.

Proceeds from the sale of bonds may be spent only to acquire or improve real property (land or buildings, structures, or fixtures and fences erected on or affixed to the land). The funds cannot be used to purchase furniture, equipment, or services necessary to open a new school.

Placing a bond issue on the ballot is not very complicated. The school board decides how much money is needed to construct schools and votes to place the measure on the local ballot. While the process is not very difficult, convincing voters to approve such a measure is a complex matter in most districts. If local resistance is strong, passing a bond initiative is next to impossible.

Capital Appreciation Bonds (CABs)

School districts found a new way to raise money for school construction in 2007; the use of Capital Appreciation Bonds or CABs. CABs are unlike typical bonds in that interest and principal payments allow districts to defer payment well into the future, as much as 40 years before payments are due.

This type of funding for school construction or modernization projects was used by hundreds of California school districts to raise over $7 billion for construction projects. The districts borrowed billions in loans with payments deferred as much as 40 years.

The general public became aware of CABs when a San Diego investigative report revealed that the Poway School District will have to pay about $1 billion for a loan of $105 million by 2051, almost ten times the amount borrowed.

In 2013, California Governor Brown signed legislation to stop the use of long-term capital appreciation bonds that can carry debt payments many times the amount borrowed. The legislation reduces the maximum maturity of CABs from 40 to 25 years and limits school district's repayment ratio to no more than four dollars in interest and principal for every dollar borrowed (Weikel, D. 2013).

Mello-Roos Community Facilities District (CFD)

In 1982 the state government approved an additional means of financing schools through the Mello-Roos Community Facilities Act. This act gave local districts authority to establish a Mello-Roos district, enabling them to raise revenue to build and maintain schools, libraries, and roads without a general tax increase. Establishing a Mello-Roos district on vacant land is possible and preferred by some developers. Residents of a Mello-Roos district are charged a fee based on their home's assessed value and the amount of funds to be raised.

A school district may go to its community to request funding of a CFD. Such a district may be formed districtwide or in a portion of the district. An advantage in some school districts is that the boundaries of the Mello-Roos district need not be contiguous with those of the school district. The necessary bonding capacity and tax rate are placed before the voters and require 2/3 approval among residents who are affected by the plan.

A second method of forming a Mello-Roos Community Facilities District is to encompass vacant land and enact a tax on development as it occurs. This method also requires the same 2/3 yes vote, but on the basis of one vote per acre of land. Where there are 12 or less property owners, as may be the case with a development under construction, a mailed ballot is allowed. A developer may prepay varying levels of the tax, thereby controlling the amount of tax to be paid by homeowners. As the homes are built and occupied, the tax activates and provides the necessary funding for school facilities. Because the tax formula is flexible and taxes need not go into effect until homes are built or occupied, developers often prefer this method for funding school construction. The cost is passed on to future home buyers in the form of annual property taxes.

On a recent successful CFD election, the district exempted properties owned by senior citizens and set different rates for homeowners of newly-constructed or newly-purchased homes. An advantage of a Mello-Roos district is elimination of Office of Local Assistance involvement, but like any approach to voters asking for higher taxes, this option requires careful planning and preparation on the part of school district and legal staff.

Parcel Tax

School districts may hold parcel tax elections to acquire funds to finance the construction of schools. A parcel tax may be variable, like a Mello-Roos assessment, or it may be a flat per-parcel amount. It may not, however, be levied in direct proportion to assessed valuation. This strategy features ease of implementation, but may be difficult to justify legally. The disadvantages are that the election must be held across the entire district and that 2/3 of the electorate must vote for approval before a parcel tax can be enacted. Between 2003 and 2017, California school districts placed 957 parcel tax propositions on the ballot; 537 passed and 420 failed (Ballotpedia, 2017).

Sales Tax

A change in state sales tax requires legislative action and the governor's approval, with no election required. Nevertheless, considering the California political climate, an increase in state sales tax is not readily obtainable. However, approval by 2/3 of the electorate may also institute a local sales tax.

Relocatable Schools

With development money so difficult to obtain and creative options limited, many districts are stretching their capital improvement dollars by purchasing relocatable classrooms. An entire school may consist of relocatable buildings: classrooms, offices, bathrooms, work areas, and cafeteria. These schools have a particular advantage in that they can be constructed in a short period of time. In some districts they have been referred to as "instant schools." While this term is not quite accurate, it is true that the timeline is considerably shortened. For one thing, relocatable classroom designs are already approved by the Office of State Architecture. Neither must an application be submitted to the State Allocation Board, a time-consuming process. The interval necessary to construct a relocatable school is certainly much shorter than the two- to seven-year period to obtain funding for and construct a permanent school.

A study conducted by the California Air Resources Board and California Department of Health Services estimated that 80 to 85 thousand portable classrooms were in use in 2003—approximately a third of all classrooms in the state. While both traditional and portable classrooms were found to have environmental problems, portables were generally in worse condition: 50% of portables had dirty air filters, their ceilings were marred by water stains (35%) or mold (3%), and 27% were too cold in the winter. Of teachers surveyed, 60% of those in portables—as compared with 23% in traditional classrooms—said they sometimes had to turn off the ventilation system because it was so noisy (Jenkins, Phillips, & Waldman, 2003).

Relocatable schools cost less than permanent structures in that the price of purchasing and preparing the site for a relocatable classroom is about $35,000 to $100,000, as compared with $115,000 to $177,000 for a permanent classroom (EdSource, 1998). On the other hand, a major disadvantage of the relocatable classroom is an increased cost for heat and air conditioning. In most cases, each unit has its own thermostat and is subject to the environmental preferences of the teacher in that classroom.

Relocatable classrooms no longer fit the 12' by 60' cramped image that characterized the trailers that have been located on many school campuses. The modern relocatable is very similar to a permanent classroom, having one or more windows, board space, and storage facilities for instructional supplies and equipment. In addition to the advantages of speedy construction and lower cost as compared to permanent buildings, a relocatable is just what the name implies—able to be moved to another location. Thus, as a district's student population shifts, relocatables can be moved from one part of the district to another. Some districts start each new school with relocatables while permanent construction is taking place on the same site. Then, when the permanent school is finished, the relocatables are moved to another site, where the process begins all over again.

Sale of Surplus Property

Districts that own surplus school sites or other surplus property may turn that real estate into an asset to provide one-time or long-term income for facility needs. State law provides that a district may sell surplus property, but if the district has capital expenditure needs, the proceeds must be used for that purpose. Alternatively, districts may lease property and may joint-venture with private entities to receive income or facilities in lieu of income.

The sale of property should be carefully reviewed by an attorney experienced in this field of law and by a competent financial advisor because certain procedures within statute may contribute to problems in converting surplus property assets into income. For example, Education Code Section 39390 may require school districts to sell surplus school property to cities at a price far below market value.

Another resource may be a valuable site that can be traded for less expensive property plus enough funds to construct a new school. For example, two Southern California districts traded or sold property that was used by the investor to construct a shopping mall and industrial complex. With proceeds from the sale of this commercial property, the districts purchased other sites and constructed new schools. Unfortunately, this is a rare circumstance, as few districts have surplus property of that value. To summarize this section, nine funding alternatives for school construction and voter requirements for each are presented in Table 7.

Table 7	Nine Funding Alternatives for School Construction and Voter Requirements

Program	Requires Voter Approval
State Lease/Purchase	No
General Obligation Bonds	Yes—55% vote
Mello-Roos (CFD)	Yes—2/3 vote
Parcel Tax	Yes—2/3 vote
Sales Tax (local)	Yes—2/3 vote
Sales Tax (state)	No
Developer Fee	No
Developer-Donated Schools	No
Certificates of Participation	No

Coalition for Adequate School Housing (CASH)

Proposition 13 prompted a group of superintendents, facility planners, architects, developers, financial institutions, attorneys, and consultants to form an organization to lobby for state funds to build schools. This organization is called the Coalition for Adequate School Housing (CASH). CASH is a statewide lobbying organization with more than 650 members. Its purpose is to develop and support new statewide bond and funding alternatives for school construction. This coalition developed an eleven-point program designed to achieve its objectives:

- School districts should have authority to pass local funding measures by majority vote
- The state should continue capital outlay funding at the current level to supplement local efforts
- Legislation should ensure that school facility needs are included in the assessment of community infrastructure needs
- The state should maintain an ample school construction fund
- Local funding should be maintained at a minimum level before state funds are made available
- The state should assume a constitutional obligation to provide minimal facilities to those districts that are unable to raise the required minimum level of local funding
- Building construction should be of high quality so that deferred maintenance is gradually phased out
- A rehabilitation program should replace the existing modernization program to update older facilities to meet Education and Building Code requirements
- Provisions should be instituted to permit construction of non-chargeable community facilities on district property
- The state should provide incentives to local school districts to seek all financial resources available, including year-round education, relocatable classrooms, and joint use of school facilities with other community agencies
- The state should continue as the primary source of funds for special housing requirements for the severely handicapped (Stork, 1992).

This program was adopted by CASH'S board of directors, and the organization has been instrumental in supporting legislation to implement the plan. CASH has also supported state bond measures for school construction.

SUMMARY

People continue to migrate to the Golden State. Many immigrants have school-age children who are knocking at the doors of the state's already overcrowded schools. Districts in growing communities are challenged to build schools in a dubious economic climate, complicated by the nation's and state's fiscal crisis, and few have viable options for school construction funding.

Providing adequate school facilities in California has become a highly complex—indeed almost impossible—task. The state needs to build 12 new classrooms and modernize 20 more each day for the next five years to keep up with the increase in student population and address substandard classrooms. The cost estimate for this construction is $11 billion.

For the past decade, the citizens of California have been asked to finance school construction by approving state facilities construction bonds. This method of financing schools has not kept pace with increases in student enrollment. The state legislative analyst also documents the ever-increasing burden of debt service.

In this chapter, several alternatives for financing school construction were discussed. Each method has several disadvantages, and for most of them, gaining citizen approval generates substantial work on the part of the staff and board of education. School construction will continue to be a major challenge for the citizens of this state in the foreseeable future.

KEY TERMS

Ad valorem tax

Assessed valuation

Building permits

CASH

COPs

Deferred Maintenance Fund

Developer-donated school

Developer fees

Facilities

Funding eligibility

GO Bonds

Impact fees

Interim facilities

Landscape and Lighting Act

Lease/purchase program

Leroy Greene Fund

Local control

Mello-Roos Community Facilities District

Office of State Architecture

Parcel Tax

Proposition 13

Proposition 46

Proposition 51

Redevelopment Agency

Relocatable classrooms

Relocatable schools

SAB

Sales tax

Williams v. California

Year-round schools

Discussion/Essay Questions

1. Until the passage of Proposition 13, General Obligation Bonds were the major source of funds for school construction. What are the major advantages and disadvantages of this type of financing?

2. Certificates of Participation (COPs) have become increasingly popular with school boards as a means of financing school construction projects. What are the pro and con arguments relative to this type of financing of school construction projects?

3. The Leroy Greene Lease/Purchase legislation has been widely used to finance school construction projects. What is the funding mechanism for this program? What are the general requirements for a district to participate in the program?

4. Several California school districts that have experienced a significant increase in student enrollment have established a Mello-Roos Community Facilities District (CFD). What are the requirements for establishing a CFD? What are its advantages and disadvantages?

References

Useful websites include the following:

California Department of Education .... http://www.cde.ca.gov
California Department of Finance .... http://www.cdf.ca.gov
California Legislative Analyst's Office .... http://www.lao.ca.gov
California Governor's Office .... http://www.governor.ca.gov
California Legislative Information .... http://www.leginfo.ca.gov
FindLaw .... http://www.findlaw.com
Fiscal Crisis Management Assistance Team .... http://www.fcmat.org

---

Abner, L. L. (2003) Professional standards for school business officials: An opportunity to reach higher levels. *School Business Affairs, 69(4)*, 4–8.

Access quality education. (2010, June). *School funding information*. Retrieved from www.schoolfundinginfo/litigation.

ACLU sues state over conditions in poor schools. (2000, May 18) *Los Angeles Times*. Retrieved from *Los Angeles Times* archives.

Agreement ends 20-year struggle to recoup special education costs. (2000, November) *California Educator 5(3)*.

American School Food Service Association. (2004) *Child nutrition programs: Legislative history highlights*. Alexandria, VA: Author. Retrieved from http://www.asfsa.org/childnutrition/govtaffairs/leghistory.asp.

ASBC (American School Bus Council) (2013). *Environment Benefits Fact: You can go green by riding yellow.* Retrieved from http://www.americanschoolbuscouncil.org/issues/environmental-benefits.

Atkinson, Andelson, Loya, Rudd & Romo. (1992, April 3) *California Supreme Court decision affirms legality of assessing a fee for home-to-school transportation* (File Reference Memo #57). San Bernardino, CA: Author.

Ballotpedia. (2011). Parcel tax elections in California. Retrieved from http://ballotpedia.org/wiki/index.php/Parcel_tax_elections_in_California.

Ballotpedia. (2017). *Parcel taxes.* Retrieved from https://ballotpedia.org/parcel-tax-elections-in-California.

Baron, K. (2013). *Future of high school exit exam unclear as California revamps testing requirements.* Retrieved from http://edsource.org/2013/future-of-high-school-exit-exam-unclear-as-california-revamps-testingrequirements.

Baron, K. (2014). *Brown touts education accomplishments, priorities in upbeat State of the State.* Retrieved from http://edsource.org/2014/brown-touts-education-accomplishments-prioritiers-in-upbeat-state-of-the-state address.

Benson, C. S. (1978) *The economics of public education* (3rd ed). Boston: Houghton Mifflin.

Bloomberg News. (2011, August 25). *Call for seat belts on buses denied.* North County Times.

Blume, H. (August 31, 2007) *L.A. Unified dishes out health benefits.* Los Angeles Times.

Blume, H. (2010, December 10). *Settlement reached on public school fees.* Los AngelesTimes, pAA3.

Boessenkool, A. (2017, September 29). Daily News. *New Law allows LAUSD - and the rest of state's schools - to donate uneaten food.* Retrieved from https://www.dailynews.com/2017/09/29/new-law-allows-lausd-and-rest-of-states-schools-to donate uneaten food.

Bohn, Danelson, Thorman. (2017). Public Policy Institute. *Child poverty in California.* Retrieved from http://www.ppic.org/publications/child-poverty-in-California.

Brennan, D. (2017, December, 16). *District Scrambles To Close Gap.* The San Diego Union-Tribune.

Buechley, D. (2017, August 24). *California voters said yes to school bonds.* Retrieved from https://www.mercurynews.com/2017/08/24/opinion-california-voters-said-ys-to-school-bonds.

Bustillos, T. A. (1989, September) Expectations held for the California school business administrator. *California Association of School Business Officials Journal, 54.*

California Lottery Commission (2017). *Unclaimed prizes,* Sacramento: CA: Retrieved from http://www.calottery.com/sitecore/content/ARCHIVE/media/fact-sheets/education.

California State Budget. (2017). *California State Budget - 2017-2018.* Retrieved from http://www.ebudget.ca-gov/Fullbudgetsummary.pdf.

California Virtual Academies. (2004) *Overview.* Simi Valley, CA: Author.

CASBO (California Association of School Business Officials). (1988) Legal aspects and accounting for student organizations and booster clubs. Workshop presented by the CASBO Professional Development Committee.

Caton, J. (1990) *The history of the American School Food Service Association: A pinch of love*. Alexandria, VA: American School Food Service Association.

Caughey, J. W. (1943) *California* (2nd ed). Englewood Cliffs, NJ: Prentice-Hall.

CCTC (California Commission on Teacher Credentialing) (2014, April). *Teacher supply in California—A report to the legislature—Annual Report—2012–2013*. Retrieved from http://www.ctc.ca.gov/reports/TS-2012-2013-annualrpt.pdf.

CDC (California Department of Corrections). (2000) *Population projections, 1995–2005*. Sacramento, CA: The Author. Retrieved from http://www.cdc.state.ca.us/pd/sooproj.pdf.

CDE (California Department of Education). (1992) *Accounting procedures for student organizations*. Sacramento, CA: Author.

CDE (California Department of Education). (2007) *California school accounting manual*. Sacramento, CA: California Department of Education. Retrieved from http://www.cde.ca.gov/fg/ac/sa/csamcomplete.asp.

CDE (California Department of Education). (2010, August 17) *General bond history—Caledfacts)*. Sacramento, CA: Retrieved from http://www.cde.ca.gov/ls/fa/sf/cefgofbondhistory.asp.

CDE (California Department of Education). (2011) Meal Programs-CalEdFacts. Sacrament, CA: Retrieved from http://www/cde/ca/gov/ls/nu/po/cefmealprog.asp.

CDE (California Department of Education) (2013). 2012–13 California High School Exit Examination Results. Retrieved from http://www.cde.ca.gov/nr/ne/yr13/yr13rel78atta.asp.

CDE (California Department of Education (2013). *California school accounting manual*. Sacramento, CA: California Department of Education. Retrieved from http://www.cde.ca.gov/fg/ac/sa/documents.csam2013complete.pdf.

CDE (California Department of Education) (2015). *Implementation of 1575*.Retrieved from cde.ca.gov/re/cp/uc/1575/20121116.asc.

CDE (California Department of Education) (2017). CalEdFacts. Retrieved from https://www.cde.ca.gov/ds/sd/cb/cdfingertipfacts.dsp.

CDE (California Department of Education) (2017) *Facts about English Learners*. Retrieved from https://www.cde.ca.gov/ds/sd/cb/cefelfacts.asp.

CDE (California Department of Education) (2017). *Second interim status report, 2017*. Retrieved from http://California Interim Status Report - 2016-2017.

CDF (California Department of Finance) (2014). California state budget 2014–15. Retrieved from http://www.ebudget.ca.gov/2014-15/pdf.

CDF (California Department of Finance) (2014). Code.org going to school in a big way. Retrieved from www.seattletimes/brierdudley/code.org-going-to-school-in-a-big-way.

CDF (California Department of Finance) (2014). Review of Transportation in California. Retrieved from www.lao.ca.gov.

CDF (California Department of Finance) (2017). *New population projections: California to surpass 50 million in 2049*. Retrieved from http://www.dof.ca.gov/research/demographics/report/estimates/e-1/document/E-1_2017.

Center for Nutrition Policy and Promotion. (1999) *Eating breakfast greatly improves schoolchildren's diet quality.* Washington, DC: U.S. Department of Agriculture. Retrieved from http://www/usda.gov/cnpp/Insights/Insights15PDF.

Chiang, J. (2007, July 5) *Controller audit reveals LAUSD owes the state $45 million.* Sacramento, CA: Retrieved from http://www.sco.ca.gov/eo/pressbox/2007/07/pr032.lausd05.pdf.

Chiang, J. (2010, June 30). *Annual Financial report of California's K-12 schools for 2009.* Retrieved from http://www.sco.ca.gov/files-AUD/k_12k_annual-rpt2008-09.pdf.

Children Now. (2002) *California, ahead on income, trails nation in education, health and economic security.* Retrieved from http://www.childrennow.org/newsroom/news-02/pr-10-23-02.cfm.

Children's Advocacy Institute. (2001) *California Children's Budget 2000–2001.* Sacramento, CA: Author.

CNN. (2017). Price of gasoline. Retrieved from http://money.CNN/pf/feaures/lists/global-gas prices.

CNN Money. (2007) *Gas prices around world.* Retrieved from http://cnnmoney.com/pf/features/lists/global_gasprices.

Collins, K. (2004) Junk food makes up quarter of U.S. diet: Large portion of calories come from nutrient-poor choices. *Nutrition Notes.* Retrieved from http://www.msnbc.com/id/5444256.

Covestor. (2011, March 16). *Gasoline prices around the word: $4 a gallon is cheap.* Retrieved from http://blog.covestor.com/2011/03/gasoline-prices-around-the-world-4-a-gallon-is-cheap.

Dechert, S. (2014, March 5). *New all-electric school bus saves California District $10,000 per year.* Retrieved from http://cleantechnica.com/2014/03/05/new-electric-school-bus-saves-california-district.

Driftmier, D. (1997, February 7) Presentation at ACSA School Business Managers Academy.

EdCal (2014, June 16). Supt. urge slow down in CCSS implementation. Association of California School Administrators.

EdCal (2017). *CTC works on teacher shortage.* The official newspaper of the Association of California School Administrators, volume 48, number 13, November 20, 2017.

Ed-Data. (2011, April). *A guide to California's school finance system.* Retrieved from http://ed-data.k12.ca.us.

Ed-Data (2013). *Understanding California's standardized testing, and reports (STAR) program.* Retrieved from http://www.ed-data.k12.ca.us.

Editorial, Los Angeles Times. (2011, May 25). *In education, free means free.* Los Angeles Times, A18.

EdSource. (1998) *California's school facilities predicament.* Palo Alto, CA: Author.

EdSource. (2017). *Governor proposes minimal increase in education budget.* https://edsource.org(2017)governor-proposes-mimimal-increase-for-k12-schools-in-next-years-budget.

Estep, L. (2008, Summer). *Rough Road-Budget, regulation take heavy toll on school transportation.* California School Business, Volume 73, number 2.

FCMAT (Fiscal Crisis & Management Assistance Team) (2014). Annual report 2012–2013. Retrieved from http://fcmat.org/wp-content/uploads/sites/4/2014/02/FCMATannual report201213.pdf.

Food Research and Action Center. (2011, March 7). *FRAC's Weekly News Digest*. Retrieved from http://org2.democracyinaction.org/o/5118/p/salsa/web/common/public/content?content_item-kEY=5216.

Food Research and Action Center (FRAC). (2014). *National school lunch program*. Retrieved from http://frac.org/federal-foodnutritiion-programs/national-school-lunch-program.

Gevertz, C. (2017). *Which states are using PARCC or smarter balanced?* Retrieved from https://www.edweek.org/ew/section/multimedia/states-using-parcc-or-smarter-balanced.html.

Gorton, R. A. (1983) *School administration and supervision* (2nd ed). Dubuque, IA: Wm. C. Brown.

Gross, S. M. (2004, March) Breakfast and lunch meal skipping patterns among fourth-grade children from selected public schools in urban, suburban, and rural Maryland. *American Dietetic Association*. Retrieved from FindArticles public database at http://www.findarticles.com.

Gunderson, G. (2004) *The National School Lunch Program: Background and development*. Food and Nutrition Services. Department of Agriculture. Retrieved from http://www.fns.uscla.gov/cnd/Lunch/AboutLunch/ProgramHistory.htm.

Hadderman, M. (1999) *School-based budgeting* (ERIC Digest No. 131). Eugene, OR: ERIC Clearinghouse on Educational Management. Retrieved from the ERIC database.

Harrison, D. (2011, March 4). *Virtual education boom hits the states*. Retrieved from http://stateline.org/live/details/story.

Hemet School District (2013). *2012–2013 Adopted Budget Report*. Retrieved from http:www.hemetusd.k12.ca.us/business/finsvcs/fiscal/budget/report.pdf.

Hirano, S. (1999, December) 25 events that shaped school transportation. *School Bus Fleet*. Retrieved from http://www.schoolbusfleet.com/ [search the archives].

Hoag, C. (2010, August 7). *ACLU probes fees charged by school districts*. North County Times, B3.

Hoffman, N. (2007, August 10). *Napa gets state's first hybrid school bus*. The Napa Valley Register. Retrieved from http://www.napavalleyregister.com/articles/2007/08/10/news/local/doc46bcca6521e51974045742.txt.

Hogo, H. (2003) *California alternative fuel incentive programs and new legislation*. Paper presented at the 9th National Clean Cities Conference, Palm Springs, CA.

Jason, S. (May, 14, 2014). Students take more classes online, but they pass fewer. Los Angeles Times, p. A5.

Jenkins, A. (2017, October). *Trump's Transportation Chief $1 billion plan again*. Retrieved from http://fortune.com/2017/10/11/trump-secretary-of-transportation.

Jenkins, P. G., Phillips, T. J., & Waldman, J. (2003) *Environmental health conditions in California's portable classrooms: Report to the California Legislature*. Sacramento, CA: California Air Resources Board & California Department of Health Services. Retrieved from http://www.arb.ca.gov/research/indoor/pcs/leg_rpt/pcs_r21.pdf.

Johnson, H. & Mejia, M. (2014). *Online learning and student outcomes in California's community colleges*. Retrieved from www.ppic.org.

Keenan & Associates. (2010, August 23). *Keenan develops robust online resource center to assist school districts in addressing special education liability and fiscal challenges*. Retrieved from http://www.keenan.com/schools/press/0901_spedPCB.asp.

KPBS (2011, June 27). *Chronically absent students cost county schools millions*. Retrieved from http://www.kpbs.org/news/2011/jun/27/chronically-absent-students-cost-county-schools-millions.

Kuhn, J. (2004) *Assessing California's charter schools*. Sacramento, CA: California Legislative Analyst's Office. Retrieved from http://lao.ca.gov/2004/charter_schools/012004_charter_schools.htm.

LAO (Legislative Analyst's Office). (2004a) *Overview of state bond debt*. Sacramento, CA: Author. Retrieved from http://www.lao.ca.gov/ballot/2004/bond_11_2004.htm.

LAO (Legislative Analyst's Office) (2013). *CalFacts—2013*. Retrieved from http://www.lao.ca.gov/reports/2013/calfacts/calfacts-010213.pdf.

Lasevoli, B. (2013, August 27). *CA getting "Smarter" with new tests to probe critical thinking*. Retrieved from http://laschoolreport.com/ca-getting-smarter-with-new-tests-to-proble-criticla-thinking.

MacVean, M. (2011, August 29). *Students grade L.A. school lunch menu*. Los Angeles Times.

NAEP. (National Assessment of Educational Progress). (2011, July). *Children and youth with disabilities*. Washington, DC: Retrieved from http://nces.ed.gov/programs/coe/indicator_cwd.asp.

NAEP (National Assessment of Educational Progress). (2015). *The nation's report card highlights 2015*. Washington, DC: Retrieved from http://nces..ed.gov/nation'sreportcard.

NAPCS (2013) (National Alliance for Public Charter Schools) (2013). Estimated number of public charter schools & students, 2013–14. Retrieved from www.publicchartes.org.

NASBO (National Association of State Budget Officers). (2017, Spring). *The fiscal survey of states*. Retrieved from http://www.nasbo.org.

National Association of State Directors of Pupil Transportation Services. (1999) *Passenger crash protection in school buses*. Retrieved from http://www.nasdpts.org/paperCrashProtect.html.

National Chamber of Commerce. (2010). *Per capita personal income by state, 1990–2010*. Retrieved from http://bber.unm.edu/econ/us-pci.htm.

National Highway Traffic Safety Administration. (2000) *Seatbelts on school buses*. Retrieved from http://www.nhtsa.dot.gov/people/injury/buses/pub/seatbelt.hmp.html.

NCES (National Center for Education Statistics). (2015). *Nations Report Card*. Retrieved from https://www.nationsreportcard.gov.profiles/stateprofile.

NCES (National Center for Education Statistics) (2017). *Projected student K-12 enrollment*. Retrieved from https://nces.ed.gov/pubs2017/2017/2017019.

NEA (National Education Association). (2017). *Rankings and Estimates: Ranking of the States (2016 and Estimates 2017)*. Washington, DC. Retrieved from http://www.nea.org/NEA-rankings and Estimates - 2016-2017.

NHTSA, (National Highway Traffic Safety Administration). (2017). *roadsafety/schoolbuses*. Retrieved from https://www.nhtsa.gov/road-safety-school buses.

Noguchi, S. (2017, July 2). K-12: *'Tidal wave of expenses' in looming California school budget crisis*. Retrieved from http://www.mercurynews.com/2017/07/02/tidal-wave-of-expenses-in-looming-california.

Nuehring, B. (2002) Preparing for the annual audit. *School Business Affairs, 68*(9), 6–8.

Occupant restraint: Seat belt history. (2004) *School Transportation News*. Retrieved from http://www.stnonline.com/stn/occupantrestraint/seatbelthistory/.

Oswalt, S. (1992) Fiscal fiascos. *Thrust for Educational Leadership, 22*(3).

Packard, L. (2010). *Lucile Packard Foundation: Annual Survey*. Retrieved from http://www.lpfh.org.

Pre-1977 U.S. school buses. (2000) *School Bus Fleet*. Retrieved from http://www.schoolbusfleet.com/SBFFB01p62.pdf.

Public Policy Institute of California. (2009, March). *Special education in California*. Retrieved from http://www.ppic.org/contents/pubs/jtf/JTF_special.jtf.pdf.

Pullmann, J. (2013). Common core issues. Retrieved from http://www.hslda.org/commoncore/hse.aspx.

Richardson, J. (2017). *The 49th annual Phi Delta Kappa/Gallup poll of the public's attitudes toward the public schools*. Bloomington, IN: Retrieved from http://pdkpoll.org/assets/downloads/PDKnational-poll-2017.pdf.

Ruskin Programme. (n.d.) *John Ruskin, 1819–1900*. Bailrigg, United Kingdom: Lancaster University. Retrieved from http://www.lancs.ac.uk/depts/ruskin/jrbiog.htm.

Rutherford, D. (2012). *Republicans vs. Democrats views on government size*. Retrieved from http://classroom.synonym.com/republicans-vs-democrats-views-government-size-7737.html.

San Diego School District, (2017). *Current Fee Schedule*. Retrieved from https://www.sandiego.gov/develoment-services/industry/information.

Savage, D. G. (1992, June 19) U.S. justices uphold Proposition 13 tax structure. *Los Angeles Times*.

Schlosser, N. (2017, December 5). *Los Angeles District Orders 2 Electric School Buses*. Retrieved from http://www.schoolbusfleet.com./news/726601/los-angeles-district-orders-2-electric-school-buses.

School Works (2014). *Developer fees*. Retrieved from http://www.schoolworksgis.com/developer-fees.html.

Scott, J. (1990) Seminar for school district and community college business office personnel and school district auditors. San Bernardino, CA.

Severson, K. (2017, September 5). New York Times. *Will the Trump Era Transform the School Lunch*. Retrieved from https?//www.nytimes.com/2017/09/05/dining/school-lunch-trump-obama.html.

Steffen, J. (2010, December 3). *School lunch bill approved in the House*. Los Angeles Times, p. A14.

Stork, F. C. (1992) Back to the drawing board. *Thrust for Educational Leadership, 21*(6): 38–41.

Tax Foundation. (2011). *2011 facts figures—How does your state compare?* Washington, DC: Retrieved from http://www.taxfoundation.org/files/ff2011.pdf.

Tustin Unified School District (2014). *Tustin Nutrition Services*. Retrieved from http://www.tustin.k12.ca.us.

Tuvalu, N. (2017, June 19). *16 southern California school districts awarded new electric school buses*. Retrieved by http://www.stnonline.com/news/latest-news.

UCCP. (University California College Prep) (2010). *Mission and history*. Retrieved from http://www.uccp.org/index.php/mission-and-history.

U.S. Bureau of the Census. (2017) Population estimates. Retrieved from http://www.census.gov

U. S. Department of Education. (2017). *Teacher Shortage Areas*. Retrieved from https://catalog.data.gov/teacher-shortage-areas-2015-2016

Wainer, H. (1993, December) Does spending money on education help? *Educational Researcher* 22(9): 22–24.

Watanabe, T. (2012, February 3). *California lawmakers keep school buses rolling*. Los Angeles Times. Retrieved from http://www.latimes.com/news/local/la-me-school-biusing-20120203,0,4896798.story.

Weeks, R. H. (1999) The first 100 days: A successful beginning as a school business administrator. *School Business Affairs*, 65(12), 22–28.

Weikel, D. (2013, October 2). *Gov. Brown signs law limiting risky capital appreciation school bonds*. Retrieved from http://articles.latimes.com/2013/oct/02/local/la-me-in-school-bonds-20131002.

West, R. (2018). *Public thinking on school choice, Common Core, higher ed, and more*. Retrieved from http://educationnext.org/2017-ednext-poll-school-reform-public-opinion-schoool-common-core.

Wigginton, B., & Hunter, K. (2004, May/June) Buckle up for the ride ahead. *Journal of School Business Management*, 69(3).

Wikipedia (2014). *Lotteries in the United States*. Retrieved from http://en.wikipedia.org/wiki/Lotteries_in_the_United States.

Winton, R. (2000, October 25) Parents sue district, seek refund of fees. *Los Angeles Times*.

Winton, R. (2001, September 29) Los Angeles: Student fees suit is nearly resolved. *Los Angeles Times*. Retrieved from *Los Angeles Times* archives.

Yang Su, E. (2011, September 2). *School bus service vanishing amid cuts*. California Watch. Retrieved from http://californiawatch.org/dailyreport/school-bus-service-vanishing-amid-ctus-12438.

Yarbrough, B. (2014, March 18). *School accountant embezzled $3m from the district by hiding lunch money in her BRA*. Retrieved from http://www.sbsun.com/general-news/201403181/alleged-lunch-money-enbezzler-judith-oakes.

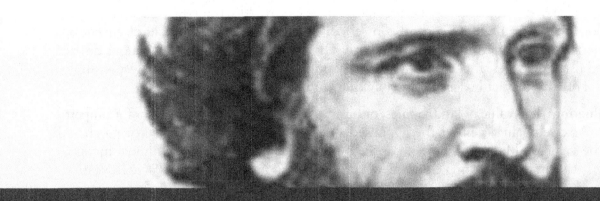

Selected School Finance Terms

The primary source of terms in this glossary is the *California School Accounting Manual* published by the California Department of Education (2003a).

Abatement: Complete or partial cancellation of an expenditure or revenue. Abatement of an expenditure is the cancellation of a part or whole of a charge previously made, usually due to refunds, rebates, or resale of materials originally purchased.

Accounts Payable: Amounts due and owed to private persons, business firms, governmental units, or others for goods received by and/or services rendered to the school district prior to the end of the fiscal year; includes amounts billed, but not yet paid.

Accounts Receivable: Amounts due and owed from private persons, business firms, governmental units, or others for goods received by and/or services rendered to them prior to the end of the fiscal year; includes amounts billed, but not received.

Accrual Basis: That method of accounting in which revenue is recorded when earned, even though not collected, and expenses are recorded when liabilities are incurred, even if not yet paid.

Ad valorem: According to value. Used in taxation for a tax related to the value. For example, property tax and sales taxes are related to the value of the property or the price paid for the merchandise.

Aid to Families with Dependent Children (AFDC): A federal assistance program that provides funds to low-income families with dependent children.

Apportionment: Allocation of state or federal aid, district taxes, or other monies among LEAs or other governmental units. The first principal apportionment (P-1) is calculated in February of the school year; the second principal apportionment, in June.

PRIMARY SOURCE: California Department of Education.

Appropriation: Funds set aside or budgeted by the state or local school district for a specific time period and specific purpose.

Assembly Bill 1200: A bill passed by the legislature and approved by the governor in 1991 that imposed major fiscal accountability controls on school districts and county offices of education. This legislation established significant administrative hurdles and obligations for school district budgeting and fiscal practices. It also gave county superintendents of schools greater responsibility for and control of local district budgets. Assembly Bill 2756 tightened these controls.

Assessed Valuation: The value of land, homes, or businesses set by the county assessor for property tax purposes. Assessed value is either the appraised value of any newly constructed or purchased property or the value on March 1, 1975, of continuously owned property, plus an annual increase. This increase is tied to the California Consumer Price Index, but may not exceed 2% each year.

Assets: School district holdings divided into two categories. The first category is cash and that which can easily be converted into cash, such as investments and accounts receivable. The second category represents costs incurred at an earlier date that have not yet been attributed to a given period, such as buildings, depreciable equipment, prepaid expenses, and deferred charges.

Audits: An examination of documents, records, and accounts to (1) determine the propriety of transactions; (2) ascertain whether all transactions are recorded properly; and (3) determine whether statements that are drawn from accounts reflect an accurate picture of financial operations and financial status for a given period of time.

Average Daily Attendance (ADA): The number of students present on each school day throughout the year, divided by the total number of school days in the school year. A school district's revenue limit income is based on its ADA.

Basic Aid: The minimum grant of $120 per K–12 pupil guaranteed by the California Constitution. The amount is included in a school district's revenue limit. It is paid even in the few instances when a district's property tax income exceeds its revenue limit.

Bilingual Education: Programs for students with limited proficiency in English. Bilingual education was essentially eliminated by Proposition 227, although parents may request bilingual instruction for their children.

Block Grant: A lump sum allocation of special purpose funds in which two or more special-purpose or categorical funds are lumped together for distribution to the state or LEA.

Bond: A certificate containing a written promise to pay a specified sum of money (called the face value) at a fixed time in the future (called the date of maturity) and specifying interest at a fixed rate, usually payable periodically.

Bonded Debt: That portion of indebtedness represented by outstanding bonds.

Bonded Debt Service: Expenditures that are incurred for interest on and redemption of bonds.

Budget: A plan of financial operation consisting of an estimate of proposed revenue and expenditures for a given period and purpose. The budget usually provides a financial plan for a single fiscal year.

Budget Act: The legislative vehicle for the state's budget appropriations. The state constitution requires that it be approved by a two-thirds vote of each house and sent to the governor by June 15 each year. The governor may reduce or delete, but not increase, individual items.

CalWORKS: A state program of financial and employment aid to families with dependent children who have income and property below established levels.

Capital Outlay: Amounts paid for the acquisition of fixed assets or additions to fixed assets. Fixed assets encompass land or existing buildings; improvements of grounds; construction, additions to, or remodeling of buildings; and initial purchases of or additions to equipment.

Capital Projects Funds: Funds established to account for financial resources that are to be used to acquire or construct major capital facilities.

Cash Flow: An analysis of expected cash receipts and cash disbursements. This analysis provides an anticipated cash balance for a given period of time and enables the district to know if it will be able to meet its financial obligations without borrowing money.

Cash in County Treasury: Cash balances on deposit in the county treasury for the various funds of the LEA.

California Basic Education Data System (CBEDS): Data collected from each district, usually in October each year. CBEDS includes statistical information about schools, teachers, and students. These data are used extensively by the California Department of Education and members of the state legislature in making decisions about public schools.

California Basic Education Skills Test (CBEST): A standardized test required of anyone seeking certification as a teacher, counselor, or administrator. The test measures proficiency in reading, writing, and mathematics.

Categorical Aid: Funds from the state or federal government granted to qualifying school districts for children with special needs, such as education of the handicapped. Funds may also be designated for special programs. Expenditures of most categorical aid funds are restricted to the purpose for which it is intended. The funds are granted to districts in addition to the revenue limit.

Certificated Employees: Employees who are required by the state to hold a credential, including full-time, part-time, substitute, and temporary teachers, counselors, and administrators.

Certificates of Participation (COPs): Documents that provide long-term financing through a lease (with an option to purchase or a conditional sale agreement). They are secured by the district's General Fund.

Chart of Accounts: A list of accounts, systematically arranged, that applies to a specific LEA. All accounts are listed in numerical order with the name of each.

Class Size Penalties: Penalties imposed on school districts that have classes in excess of prescribed maximum sizes. Class size penalties result in a reduction in ADA which, in turn, results in a loss in revenue limit income. Education Code 41376 contains the class size limitations.

Classified Employees: School employees who are not required to hold teaching credentials, such as secretaries, custodians, bus drivers, food service workers, instructional aides, and some management personnel. The latter may include, for example, chief accountants, transportation directors, and directors of food service programs.

Clearing Accounts: Accounts used to accumulate total receipts or expenditures for later distribution among the accounts to which such receipts or expenditures are properly allocable.

Collective Bargaining: A process for negotiations between management and employees regarding salary and working conditions. Senate Bill 160, approved by the legislature in 1975, defines the manner and scope of negotiations between school districts and employee organizations.

Consumer Price Index (CPI): A measure of the cost of living compiled by the United States Bureau of Labor Statistics. These indices of inflation are calculated regularly for the United States, California, some regions within California, and selected cities. The CPI is one of several measures of economic change.

Contingent Liabilities: Items that may become liabilities as a result of conditions undetermined at a given date; e.g., guarantees, pending lawsuits, judgements and appeals, and unsettled claims.

Contra Account: An account to record offsetting transactions; e.g., abatements.

Contracted Services: Services and all related expenditures rendered under contract by personnel who are not on the payroll of the LEA.

Cost of Living Adjustment (COLA): An increase in funding for revenue limits or categorical programs. Current law ties COLAs to various indices of inflation, although different amounts are appropriated in some years.

Current Expense of Education: The current General Fund operating expenditures of an LEA for kindergarten and grades one through twelve, excluding expenditures for food services, community services, non-agency activities, fringe benefits for retired persons, facilities acquisition and construction.

Current Liabilities: Amounts due and payable for goods and services received prior to the end of the fiscal year. Current liabilities should be paid within a short period of time, usually less than a year.

Debt Service Funds: Funds established to account for accumulation of resources for, and payment of, general long-term debt principal and interest.

Deferred Maintenance: Major repairs of buildings and equipment that have been postponed by school districts. Some matching state funds are available to districts that establish a deferred maintenance program.

Deficit: The amount by which a sum of money falls short of a required amount (e.g., apportionment deficits).

Deficit Fund Balance: Within a fund, the excess of liabilities over assets.

Deficit Spending: The excess of actual expenditures over actual revenues (also referred to as an operating deficit).

Developer Fees: A specified charge per square foot on new residential and commercial construction. Developer fees are levied by school districts to generate revenues to build or renovate schools. Proceeds are used to build or renovate schools or for portable classrooms.

Direct Support Charges: Charges for a support program and services that directly benefit other programs.

Discretionary Funds: Funds allocated to a district or school that can be spent at district or site discretion.

Economic Impact Aid (EIA): State categorical aid for districts with concentrations of children who are bilingual, transient, or from low-income families.

Education Code: The body of law that regulates education in California. Additional regulations are contained in the California Administrative Code, Title 5; Government Code; and general statutes.

Education Department General Administrative Regulations (EDGAR): The regulations of the U.S. Department of Education incorporating certain circulars from the Office of Management and Budget.

Employee Benefits: Amounts paid by the LEA on behalf of employees. These amounts are over and above an individual's gross salary; they are fringe benefit payments. While not paid directly to employees, benefits nevertheless account for a portion of personnel costs. Examples are (1) group health or life insurance payments, (2) contributions to employee retirement, (3) OASDI (social security) taxes, (4) workers' compensation payments, and (5) payments made to personnel on sabbatical leave.

Encroachment: The expenditure of a school district's general purpose funds for special purpose programs, such as special education or transportation. Encroachment occurs in most districts that provide services for handicapped children. Other common examples of encroachment include student food services and student transportation.

Encumbrances: Obligations in the form of purchase orders, contracts, salaries, and other commitments chargeable to an appropriation and for which a part of the appropriation is reserved.

Enterprise Funds: Funds used to account for those ongoing LEA activities that, because of their income-producing character, are similar to activities in the private sector.

Equalization: Funds allocated by the legislature to raise districts with lower revenue limits toward the statewide average.

Expenditures: The costs of goods delivered or services rendered, whether paid or unpaid, including expenses, provision for debt retirement not reported as a liability of the fund from which retired, and capital outlay.

Fidelity Bond: A form of insurance that provides for indemnification of the LEA or other employer for losses arising from theft by or dishonesty of employees.

Fiscal Crisis Management Assistance Team (FCMAT): A committee formed within the California Department of Education to review and redesign financial reporting forms for all school districts. The FCMAT accounting system was required of all districts and county offices of education as of the 1988–89 school year.

Fiscal Year: A period of one year, the beginning and the ending dates of which are fixed by statute. In California, the fiscal year begins on July 1 and ends on June 30.

Fixed Assets: Assets of a permanent character having continuing value; e.g., land, buildings, machinery, furniture, and equipment.

Full-time equivalent: The ratio derived by dividing the number of work hours required in a part-time position by the number of work hours required in a corresponding full-time position.

Fund: A fiscal and accounting entity with a self-balancing set of accounts recording cash and other financial resources, together with all related liabilities and residual equities or balances, and changes therein, which are segregated to carry on specific activities or attain certain objectives in accordance with applicable regulations, restrictions, or limitations.

Fund Balance: The difference between assets and liabilities; the fund equity of governmental and trust funds.

Gann Spending Limit: A ceiling, or limit, on each year's appropriation of tax dollars by the state, cities, counties, school districts, and special districts. Districts are permitted to increase budgets equal to inflation—that is, equal to the change in the Consumer Price Index or per capita personal income, whichever is smaller—or changes in the district's ADA. Proposition 111, adopted in June 1990, amended the Gann inflation factor to equate only to the change in per capita personal income.

General Fund: The fund used to finance the ordinary operations of the LEA. It is available for any legally authorized purpose.

General Obligation Bonds: Bonds for capital outlay, financed through taxes. Elections to authorize General Obligation Bonds in a school district must be approved by a 55% vote. State measures only require a majority vote.

Generally Accepted Accounting Principles (GAAP): Uniform minimum standards of, and guidelines for, financial accounting and reporting. These accounting principles govern the form and content of the basic financial statements of an entity. They encompass the conventions, rules, and procedures necessary to define accepted accounting practices at a particular time. They include not only broad guidelines of general application, but also detailed practices and procedures. Generally accepted accounting principles provide a standard against which to measure financial presentations. The primary authoritative source on application of these principles to state and local governments is the Governmental Accounting Standards Board (GASB).

Grants-in-Aid: Outright donations or contributions, usually by a superior governmental unit, without prior establishment of conditions with which the recipient must comply.

Holding Accounts: Suspense accounts that are used temporarily to accumulate costs that will ultimately be charged to other programs.

Income: A term used in accounting for a proprietary fund type to represent the excess of revenues earned over the expenses incurred in carrying on the fund's operations. The term "income" should not be used in lieu of revenue in governmental-type funds.

Indirect Cost and Overhead: Elements of cost necessary in operating an LEA or in performing a service that are of such nature that the amount applicable to each accounting unit cannot be determined readily and accurately or for which the cost of such determination exceeds the benefit of the determination.

Indirect Support Charges: Charges for routine services not performed as a special service for a particular program, but allocated to using programs.

Interfund Transfers: Money that is taken from one fund under the control of the governing board and added to another fund under the board's control. Interfund transfers are not revenues or expenditures of the LEA; they simply move dollars from one fund to another.

Internal Audit: An appraisal activity within an LEA that (1) determines the adequacy of the system of internal control, (2) verifies and safeguards assets, (3) determines the reliability of the accounting and reporting system, (4) ascertains compliance with existing policies and procedures, and (5) appraises the performance of activities and work programs.

Internal Control: A plan of organization under which employees' duties are so arranged and records and procedures so designed as to provide a system of self-checking, thereby enhancing accounting control over assets, liabilities, revenue, and expenditures. Under such a system employees' work is subdivided so no one employee performs a complete cycle of operation; such procedures call for proper authorization by designated officials.

Intrabudget Transfers: Amounts transferred from one appropriation account to another within the same fund.

Inventory: A detailed list showing quantities and description of property on hand at a given time. It also may include units of measure, unit prices, and values.

J-200, J-380: Financial and program cost accounting reports submitted by districts and county offices to the California Department of Education. The information is used to monitor the fiscal conditions of districts.

LEP (Limited-English-Proficient): LEP students are those who do not have fluent English language skills (i.e., comprehension, speaking, reading, and writing) necessary to succeed in the school's regular instructional program. LEP includes non-English-speaking and limited-English-proficient students.

Lease-Purchase Agreements: Contractual agreements that are termed "leases," but, in substance, amount to purchase contracts.

Liabilities: Legal obligations (with the exception of encumbrances) that are unpaid.

Life Span (grade span): Broad group classification of students according to age and school progress, i.e., preformal, elementary, secondary, and adult.

Local Educational Agency (LEA): The local school district.

Lottery: A game of chance approved by California voters in 1984. A minimum of 34% of lottery revenues is distributed to public schools and colleges and must be used for education of pupils.

Maintenance Assessment Districts: School districts acting under legislation that permits charging property owners a fee for improvement of school playgrounds and athletic fields. Districts may impose the "fee" by a vote of the local governing board, but the district must show a benefit to each fee payer.

Mandated Costs: School district expenditures that occur as a result of federal or state law, court decisions, administrative regulations, or initiative measures. School districts are eligible to apply for state funds to reimburse these costs.

Mega-Item: Block funding for selected categorical programs. The procedure was initiated in 1992–93 and allows districts to redirect a portion of categorical funds from one categorical program to another.

Mello-Roos: A community facilities district that can be established by a two-thirds vote to issue bonds and levy local taxes for school construction.

Mentor Teacher: A specially selected teacher who receives a stipend to work with new and experienced teachers on curriculum and instruction.

Migrant Education: Special funds for districts with students who are children of migrant workers.

Modified Accrual Basis: The accrual basis of accounting adapted to the governmental fund type. Under it, revenues are recognized when they become both "measurable" and "available" to finance expenditures of the current period. Most expenditures are recognized (recorded) when the related liability is incurred.

Multi-year Financial Plan: A plan that presents in tabular form financial estimates of program costs over a period of years. These estimates should reflect future financial impact of current decisions. The data in the plan should be organized to be consistent with program structure.

Necessary Small School: An elementary school with less than 101 ADA or a high school with less than 301 ADA that meets the standards for "necessary."

Object: As used in an expenditure classification, a term that applies to the article purchased or the service obtained.

Parcel Tax: A special tax that is not *ad valorem* (proportional to the value of the property). Usually the tax is for a specific purpose. Parcel taxes must be approved by local two-thirds vote.

Permissive Override Tax: A tax authorized prior to Proposition 13, allowing a school district governing board to levy a special tax for the improvement of education. Districts are no longer allowed to levy such taxes.

Prepaid Expenses: Items for which payment has been made, but from which benefits have not been realized as of a certain date; e.g., prepaid rent, prepaid interest, and premiums on unexpired insurance.

Prior Year's Taxes: Tax revenues that were delinquent in a prior year and are received in the current fiscal year. In the revenue limit formula, these revenues offset state aid for the current year.

Property Taxes: Taxes based on ownership of property and measured by its value. Property taxes include both general property taxes (i.e., relating to property as a whole, real or personal, tangible or intangible, whether taxed at a single rate or at classified rates) and special property taxes (i.e., on selected types of property, such as motor vehicles or certain or all tangibles, subject to rates that are not directly related to rates applying to general property taxation).

Proposition 13: An initiative amendment passed in 1978 adding Article XIII A to the California Constitution. Tax rates on secured property are restricted to a maximum of one percent of full cash value. Proposition 13 also defined assessed value and requires a 2/3 vote to change existing taxes or levying of new taxes.

Public Employees' Retirement System (PERS): A California state retirement system established for state employees. California school classified employees are members of PERB.

Public Employment Relations Board (PERB): A board of five persons appointed by the governor to regulate collective bargaining between school employers and employee organizations.

Range: The difference between the highest and lowest values in a group of data.

Real Property: Property consisting of land, buildings, minerals, timber, landscaping, and all improvements thereto.

Regional Occupational Center or Program (ROC/P): A vocational education program for high school students and adults. An ROC or ROP may be operated by a single district, by a consortium of districts under a joint powers agreement, or by a county office of education for districts within that county.

Registered Warrant: A warrant that is registered by the county treasurer for future payment because of present lack of funds. Registered warrants are to be paid with interest in the order of their registration.

Reserves: Funds set aside in a school district budget to provide for future expenditures or to offset future losses, for working capital, or for other purposes.

Restricted Funds: Monies whose use is restricted by legal requirements or by a donor. These funds can only be spent for a specific purpose or program. Funds received in excess of the expenditures in any one year must be carried over to the next year for that program or returned to the donor (state or other source of funds).

Revenue Limit: The specific amount of state and local taxes a school district may receive per pupil for its general education program. Annual increases are determined by the legislature. Categorical aid is allocated in addition to the revenue limit.

Revenues: Increases in fund financial resources other than interfund transfers or debt issue proceeds. Revenues are the primary financial resource of a fund. Revenues are recognized when assets are increased without increasing liabilities or incurring an obligation to repay expenditures.

Revolving Cash Fund: A stated amount of money used primarily for emergency or small disbursements and reimbursed periodically through properly documented expenditures, which are summarized and charged to proper accounting classifications.

School Improvement Program (SIP): Money granted by the state to selected schools to carry out a plan developed by the school site council for improvement of the school's program.

School Site Council: Parents, students, teachers, and other staff selected by their peers to prepare a school improvement plan and to assist in seeing that planned activities are carried out and evaluated.

Scope of Bargaining: The range of subjects negotiated between school districts and employee organizations during the collective bargaining process. Scope includes matters relating to wages, hours, and working conditions. PERB is responsible for interpreting disputes as to matters that are or are not within scope.

Second Period Attendance (P-2): The period of time from July 1 through the last full school month ending on or before April 15. Revenue limit sources are based on ADA generated during this period.

Secured Roll: Assessed value of real property, such as land, buildings, secured personal property, or anything permanently attached to land, as determined by each county assessor.

Senate Bill 90: Finance legislation approved by the legislature and signed by the governor in 1972. This legislation established the revenue limit system for funding school districts. The first revenue limit amount was determined by dividing the district's 1972–73 state and local income by that year's ADA (average daily attendance, at that time including excused absences). This per-ADA amount is the historical base for all subsequent revenue limit calculations.

Senate Bill 813: Education reform legislation approved by the legislature and signed by the governor in 1983. This legislation contained a series of "reforms" in funding calculations, as well as in programs. Longer day, longer year, mentor teachers, and beginning teacher salary adjustment are a few of the programs implemented by SB 813.

Serrano v. Priest: A California Supreme Court decision that declared the system of financing schools unconstitutional because it violated the equal protection clause of the state's constitution. The court said that by 1980 the relative effort, or tax rate, required of taxpayers for local schools must be nearly the same throughout the state and that differences in annual per-pupil expenditures due to local wealth must be less than $100.00. The impact of Proposition 13 settled the taxpayer equity provision.

Shortfall: An insufficient allocation of money, requiring an additional appropriation or resulting in deficits.

Split Roll: A system for taxing business and industrial property at a different rate from individual homeowners.

Squeeze Formula: The formula used from 1973–1974 through 1981–1982 to calculate the annual inflation increase in the base revenue limit. This calculation provided smaller-than-average increases to high-revenue districts, thus "squeezing" their revenues as a means of accomplishing revenue equalization. Effective in 1983–1984 the squeeze formula was eliminated; since then, all districts of the same type now receive the same dollar inflation increase.

State Allocation Board (SAB): A regulatory agency that controls most state-aided capital outlay and deferred maintenance projects and distributes funds for them.

State School Fund: A fund to which the state appropriates money each year. The monies are then used to make state aid payments to school districts. Section A of the State School Fund is for K–12 education; Section B, for community college education.

State Teachers' Retirement System (STRS): A state retirement system for teachers and other certificated employees. State law requires certificated employees, school districts, and the state to contribute to this retirement system.

Stores: Goods that are on hand in storerooms and subject to requisition.

Sunset: The termination of regulations for a categorical program. A schedule for the legislature to consider the sunset of most state programs is in current law. The law was intended to ensure the evaluation of programs on a regular time interval so those no longer useful could be discontinued.

Tax Anticipation Notes: Notes issued in anticipation of collection of taxes, usually retirable only from tax collections and frequently only from the proceeds of the tax levy whose collection they anticipate.

Tax Relief Subventions: Funds ordinarily paid to compensate for taxes lost because of tax relief measures.

Tenure: A system of due process and employment guarantee for teachers. After serving a two-year probation period, teachers are assured continued employment in the school district unless very carefully defined procedures for dismissal or layoff are successfully followed.

Tidelands Oil Revenues: Money for oil on state-owned lands. When available, some of the revenues are appropriated for K–12 capital outlay needs or other special purposes.

Transfer: Interdistrict or interfund payments or receipts not chargeable to expenditures or credited to revenue. Certain budget revisions are often referred to as transfers.

Unencumbered Balance: That portion of an appropriation or allotment not yet expended or obligated.

Unification: Joining together of all or part of an elementary school district (K–6 or K–8) and high school district (7–12 or 9–12) to form a new unified school district (K–12) with a single governing board.

Unified School District: A school district serving students from kindergarten through 12th grade.

Unrestricted Funds: Funds received for the general education of students. These funds are also used for support costs necessary to operate a school district. The majority of unrestricted revenues come from the revenue limit calculation that is based on the district's ADA. Lottery funds are also unrestricted.

Unsecured Roll: Assessed value of personal property other than secured property.

Urban Impact/Meade Aid: State aid to large, metropolitan districts and to qualifying high school and their feeder elementary districts. The money carries no restrictions on its use. This legislation was approved on the assumption that the cost of education is higher in a metropolitan area than elsewhere.

Vouchers: Coupons issued by a state to individual children for admission to school and redeemed by those schools for cash. A voucher system could include public as well as private school students.

Waiver: Permission from the California Board of Education in response to the request of a school district to set aside the requirements of an Education Code provision.

Work Order: A written authorization for performance of a particular job. A work order describes the nature and location of the job and specifies the work to be performed. Such authorizations are usually assigned job numbers, and provision is made for accumulating and reporting labor, material, and other costs.

INDEX